SOUL ON THE STREET

In this extraordinary personal autobiography, William gives us an insight into what it has been like to play Ken for all those years. He tells the story of his early life and the spiritual influences that have inspired him to seek a deeper understanding of life. His years in the Army shaped him into a responsible and self-reliant young man who realised at the end of his service as an officer that he wanted to act. William also talks about how he has dealt with his various personal challenges, including the profound impact of the tragic loss of his young daughter.

SOUL ON THE STREET

SOUL ON THE STREET

by

William Roache

Magna Large Print Books
Long Preston, North Yorkshire,
BD23 4ND, England.

British Library Cataloguing in Publication Data.

Roache, William
        Soul on the street.

        A catalogue record of this book is
        available from the British Library

        ISBN   978-0-7505-2951-8

First published in Great Britain in 2007 by
Hay Publishing UK Ltd.

Copyright © William Roache, 2007

Cover illustration © mirrorpix

The moral rights of the author have been asserted

Published in Large Print 2009 by arrangement with
Hay House UK Ltd.

Magna Large Print is an imprint of Library Magna Books Ltd.

Printed and bound in Great Britain by
T.J. (International) Ltd., Cornwall, PL28 8RW

To my daughter Edwina

*My fear of death and my fear of infinity
caused me to seek truth and understanding.
I am eternally grateful to them.*

CONTENTS

Acknowledgements

I would like to thank my wife Sara and all my family for their love, patience and support.

Lizzie Hutchins for all her hard work in bringing some order to this book.

Chris Hutchins who instinctively knows the true shape of any work, as a sculptor will look at a piece of stone and see the perfect shape within, for his encouragement and good work.

All at Hay House for the warmth with which I was welcomed, the understanding and professionalism that I was given and the peace of mind that comes with knowing that you are in the right hands.

And Dr Thomas Maugham and Peggy Kennard for their guidance and for passing on their great wisdom.

Preface

For me the year 2000 was one of momentous personal events. In the February I went to Buckingham Palace to receive my MBE from the Queen and before the year ended my daughter Verity had won her place at St Andrew's University where she joined Prince William reading art history.

But it was an event which did not get into the newspapers for which I remember the year most vividly. Sifting one morning through the pile of letters I get each day from the people who watch *Coronation Street*, I spotted an envelope addressed in a familiar handwriting. I opened it immediately, anxious to know what the writer had to say this time. I was not disappointed – the letter contained a message from my daughter Edwina. The messenger, whose handwriting I had come to know so well, was the medium Peggy Kennard.

Edwina – as you will read in greater detail in Chapter 12, *Love and Loss* – had been taken from us when she was just 18 months old. She had died in her cot at the home my wife Sara and I shared in Sara's home town of Wilmslow in Cheshire.

Peggy's letters were always very special to me. She sent them to my workplace – the Granada Television studios in Manchester – my dressing room there was (and still is) one of my sanctuaries, a place where I can be utterly alone, isolated from the outside world. That and my conservatory at home have long been the grown-up equivalent of the dens I used to build as a child, places where I could be by myself with only my thoughts for company.

I am a person who can easily be moved to tears on certain occasions and this was one of those. Peggy wrote to tell me that Edwina wanted Sara and me to know that she was well and happy on the Other Side and busy working as a nurse, helping small children who had died and woken up in the next world crying for their mothers in this.

I had absolutely no doubt about the validity of the message. Peggy had been writing to me since she saw me discussing spiritual matters on the Sunday morning television pro-gramme *Heaven & Earth*. Astonishing though it may seem in view of our closeness, we never met and I rarely spoke to her on the telephone, but from my study of all things spiritual, I know instinctively when a medium is a good one. Peggy's messages always carried the sort of information which proved to me that she was special and had a channel to the Other Side that few could match. She was a wonderful person without a selfish bone in her body or an untruthful thought in her head, and I often discussed my problems in the letters I exchanged with her as she passed on guidance for me from the spirit world, so I was filled with joy when she told me verbatim what my daughter had had to say.

Edwina had prefaced her message with the words, 'I want to speak to my father whom I know you love' and she concluded it with the phrase 'Love, always love'. How moving is that?

My understanding is that pretty soon after death we reach the full state of being we had before we arrived in this world, so it came as no surprise to me that, despite her tender age when she had passed sixteen years earlier, Edwina was now able to operate as what we, on this side, would call an adult.

My tears welled up as I read the letter again and again before it was time to put it to one side and change into the *Coronation*

Street clothes wardrobe had laid out for me. Then I became Ken Barlow once again and Bill Roache's tears had to be dried. A last-minute look at the dressing room table reminded me to place the wedding ring on my finger (Ken wears one, Bill doesn't) before I stepped out on to the set where the likes of Rita Fairclough, Vera and Jack Duckworth, Blanche Hunt and my on-off wife Deirdre were already at their stations in the bar of the Rover's Return.

In the 47 years I have been in the show I have hardly ever discussed with my fellow actors the spiritual beliefs which I have laced through this autobiography and which are such an important part of my story. As you will discover, there are huge differences between the real world that I have recorded as honestly as I can on these pages, and the world of make-believe, which Ken Barlow inhabits. Although more than 20 years have elapsed since she passed, our beloved Edwina is very much a part of what I know to be the real world...

Introduction

This is a casual saunter through my life, touching on the events that helped shape my spiritual understanding. I hope it will help people who are searching for meaning in their lives and don't know where to look. Maybe it will help them forward a little. That's my hope.

My early life was overshadowed by two fears, one more understandable than the other, and they were the fears of death and of infinity. It may seem strange, but I am grateful to both of them. It was the fear of death that drove me to search beyond the normal channels for the truth about life after death and it was the fear of infinity that showed me there was more to life than could be understood by our finite minds. They were very real fears at the time – the awful dread that one day everything would be over turned me into a hypochondriac at an early age – if I had a bump on my leg it had to be cancer. Nowadays there would be a counsellor for that kind of problem but back then you sorted yourself out ... or not.

I always felt that I had a mission in life, something that I had to do. I wanted to serve and help people and to do this I needed a better understanding of who we are and why we're here. For me the greatest question in life was always, *What is the purpose of it all?*

I was seeking answers from an early age, but for a long while I was unable to find any that satisfied me. I know that many people find themselves in a similar situation. Nowadays I often get letters from people who don't know where to turn for information.

The best place to look is within. Each of us is on an individual journey and each of us will find our own answers. So I always write back and say, 'As you go to sleep, say to God, or the universe, or your higher self, "Help me to understand." If you keep repeating that, sooner or later something will cross your path that will give you the answer. It can be anything from a person to a headline, or even just a thought, but you will recognize it when it's there in front of you.'

I know that if you ask for understanding, you will get it, because it has happened to me. Sometimes the results have been quite magical.

I belong to no religion, philosophy or

group, but would call myself a seeker for the truth. The views that I am putting forward are mine and my understanding of the great truths. If there is anything in these pages that offends your reason, just leave it. That's fine. My hope is simply that anyone who is on a similar journey to mine will find this helpful.

I have now lived quite a long time and I feel I haven't advanced as far as I should have done. But if you don't have that feeling, you won't continue to move forward. It is what drives us on. So I know I will always be searching, always seeking greater knowledge and understanding.

To further my knowledge I read a lot of esoteric books. I'm really interested in those by teachers from the spiritual realms, people like Silver Birch and White Eagle and books like *In Tune with the Infinite*. These books are really the only ones I want to read. I could read them all the time; the words are just beautiful. Some of the phrases that have meant a lot to me are scattered throughout this book. Sometimes I have noted their origin; mostly I have not. Often I have taken a phrase and made it my own, changing the words slightly. I often pick out something that strikes me and keep it in my mind throughout the day, almost like a mantra, pondering on it and searching for new insights. A simple little sentence can have so many different meanings at different times. I hope that these words will help you, too.

My search for the great truths of life remains highly important to me. If we all understood our spiritual nature and what happens after death, it would very much affect, for the better, the way we live our lives, and what could be more important than that?

Part I

Death and Infinity

'Where we find ourselves is the
place ordained by God.
We are to be masters of our circumstances.'

CHAPTER 1

Rutland House

*'A journey of a thousand miles
starts with a single step.'*
Lao Tzu

There is something mysterious about my arrival in this world: according to my birth certificate, I was born on 25 April 1932, though until I was 18, when the certificate was dug out of a cupboard for a passport application, I always celebrated my birthday on the 23rd. Rather surprisingly, I thought, my parents didn't remember the date of the big event. I wrote down 25th on the application form but carried on celebrating on the 23rd.

Whenever it was, I was born in Ilkeston, a small Derbyshire mining town. My grandfather and father were both doctors and it was expected that there would be a third brass plate on the gatepost of Rutland House, which combined the family home with the surgery and waiting rooms of the general practice.

My grandfather, William, had moved into the house at the end of the nineteenth century and practised there until his early death in the mid-'20s. It was a large, early Victorian house set in an extensive garden with two very big marble pillars at the front door. A conservatory was attached to one side of the house and an old cottage to the other. On the ground floor of the cottage there was an ancient well covered by a square flagstone with a metal ring in the centre. As a child, it fascinated me and I was always wanting to look down it. The joke was that this was where the doctors hid their mistakes.

The conservatory, which had a fruitful grapevine, was also the entrance to the surgery waiting room and provided extra seating on busy nights. My grandfather, who was much loved by his patients, encouraged them to eat the grapes while they were waiting, which they did in grateful moderation. I fear a similar offer made today would result in someone turning up with a supermarket trolley and taking the lot.

'The greatest service we can do for another is to help him to help himself.'

Although we missed each other by quite a few years, I feel a great affinity with my grandfather. He was a very compassionate man and would often be called out simply to settle a family argument. I remember being told that during the General Strike of 1926 he would visit people and when he left there would be a half-crown, which was quite a lot of money in those days, left on the table for them. That's the kind of man he was.

As my father later told me, he also had a profound interest in spiritual matters. He was a Freemason, a hypnotist, a Theosophist, a Spiritualist, a homoeopath and an esotericist with a special interest in Rudolf Steiner. In many ways he was decades ahead of his time. He was what we would now call 'New Age'. He would spend many evenings with the local vicar, the Reverend Butterton, drinking claret and debating metaphysical matters until the early hours. He gave half of the garden of Rutland House to the Rudolf Steiner Society to build a school. Steiner was an esoteric philosopher with an extraordinary insight into the spiritual realms. He was also a homoeopath and an educationalist with unorthodox views. So Michael House School, built in the classic

Steiner style with the minimum of straight lines and corners, became our new neighbour. He believed that schools should be a place of joy. There was no shouting and none of the pupils misbehaved because there was nothing to rebel against.

My father had no interest or involvement in any of these things and so a generation was skipped. Once when I tried to discuss some spiritual matter with him I remember him saying with some amazement that I was talking just like his father.

When I was growing up our household consisted of my parents, Vincent and Hester, my sister, Beryl, who was three years older than me, a maid and a doctor who was my father's assistant. Various other relatives stayed from time to time and we always had a cat and a dog as well.

Rutland House was an interesting and mainly enjoyable place for a child. The garden was a particular joy, with a beautiful weeping ash tree embracing a swing and a sandpit. My sister and I spent a lot of time there. There were also lawns, rockeries, flowerbeds, a kitchen garden, a greenhouse, two garages and a small rough wooded area. We had a gardener, Mr Beardsley, an old red-haired man who always wore a bowler hat.

I also loved the house itself. My mother used to ask me why, because in her view it was a lot of work. It was hard for her to keep it clean. I remember on washdays she used to get the old tubs out and the mangle, and the maid and my mother would be working away pounding the clothes and hanging everything out to dry. It was hard work.

The house was also cold – there was no central heating and it was a big house. We had an old hearth and at night firebricks would be laid in it and when the fire died out, we'd each take a firebrick, wrap it in a blanket and take it upstairs to put in our beds to warm them. I used to suffer from leg ache – I'd wake up with my legs aching and my mother would come out and get a hot towel and put it round them. The bedrooms were usually damp and often the bedclothes were too.

We cooked on an oven over the fire in the hearth and my mother was always boiling up an old ham bone or making soup out of something. There was always some bit of food being reheated. One Christmas when I was around two or three, the oven door had been left open for a while before the fire was lit and the cat got in. Then the door was closed, the fire was lit and the cat was shut inside. We couldn't hear it crying. That was awful. It died. I don't remember the actual event, but I remember being told the story. Everyone was horrified.

I was born during the Depression, when people often had very little. Mining areas suffered particularly badly at that time. Ours was a middle-class household, but my mother was always quite frugal, always making do. There was no waste, no throwing things away. You repaired everything. You had little segs you could nail into your shoes to prevent them wearing out, leather patches on the elbows of your jackets, and you mended the inner tube of your bike. In short, you learned how to improvise, how to keep things going. You never bought anything new unless you had to. It was a very big change in your life, in fact, when you did.

My mother herself had had a very tough childhood. She was very artistic and musical and would have loved to have gone to art school or music school, but her father, Albert, who was something of a drinker, would have none of it. Instead she had to work in the family shop in Blackpool from the age of 14. It sold ice cream and sweets, and it was there that she met my father. He was about 16 or 17 at the time and had had rheumatic fever and been sent to Blackpool to convalesce. He used to ride past the shop on his bicycle and he caught my mother's eye. He never came into the shop, but there was a big lamppost outside with a ledge on it and one day he put a note on it, asking her to meet him on the promenade. She went, taking a friend along as a chaperone, and he gave her a box of chocolates. This romantic gesture didn't quite work out, though, because she didn't dare eat them as she thought they might be drugged! It took several years after the box of chocolates before they started courting properly, but my father used to go back to Blackpool every year to see her. She was very strictly controlled by her parents and she wasn't really allowed out, but my father was going to be a medical student at St Bartholomew's in London and so later on her family encouraged the match.

Just as my father was qualifying, about two or three months before he took his finals, his father died, followed three days later by his mother, both of influenza. So my father had to take over the practice before he really had any practical experience at all. His father had left him a pile of debts and his younger brother, John, was just starting to study medicine at Bart's and was living off an allowance paid for by the family. On his deathbed, my grandfather made my father promise to look after John. So he quickly settled down, got married and took on the practice.

My father was a conscientious man and worked terrifically hard. In those days there was no National Health Service and a general practitioner was on call round the clock and also did his own dispensing. The cellar at Rutland House was full of shelves and cupboards laden with all the various liquids and powders from which my father made up his prescriptions. Once they were ready he would place them on a table in the hall, ready for collection, alongside a slate with the names and addresses of the house calls he had to make.

Uncle John, meanwhile, continued to live off the family allowance while studying at St Bartholomew's. After about four years he told my father he had failed his finals for the second time and needed to stay on for another year. My father contacted the medical school and was astonished to find Uncle John had in fact been sent down three years earlier. All that time he had been blowing his allowance in London. Not only that, he had become an alcoholic – my grandmother had apparently been one too, so perhaps a family weakness was handed down. I remember as a teenager going to a dance at Ilkeston Town Hall and seeing him swaying in the middle of the floor with an inane grin on his face before he simply fell over. I can also remember finding heaps of empty booze bottles in a room at the end of Rutland House where my father kept a workbench.

Whatever the case, something had to be done, and the family took matters in hand. Uncle John was engaged at the time to a young lady called Molly. That was broken off and Reverend Butterton was persuaded to write a glowing reference to get him into the army. He was accepted by the Royal Medical Corps and my parents breathed a sign of relief.

I believe we all plan our lives before we incarnate. Each soul decides where it is going to – where it will live and the family it will be born into. So this was the family I had chosen. We are all eternal beings and we are here to learn certain lessons. The family we are born into will be part of that. Each person in the family has something to teach us. We all learn from each other. We may have made certain agreements with each other before incarnating, deciding to play certain roles in each other's lives. It is all meticulously planned and nothing is overlooked and nothing is missed.

To me, reincarnation is the only thing that makes sense of the apparent unfairness of birth. Otherwise, how do you account for a child that's born into poverty in Ethiopia and dies of AIDS at two or three? Or children born into violent circumstances rather than to millionaires to enjoy lives of luxury? If this life is a one-off, where is the fairness in that? One person may be born into a tribe in Africa where there's no education or facilities and another may be born into a family which can send them to university – where is the fairness in that? But when you understand about reincarnation, you understand that we are all spiritual beings undergoing experiences that are right for us at this time in our development. A soul will always choose the environment that suits its particular needs in that particular incarnation. And through reincarnation we move upwards in terms of consciousness and understanding and environment and education. This world, in effect, was created as a schoolroom, a place for all of us to learn and grow until we progress to other worlds and spheres of activity.

Until our consciousness is high enough we are born into the level of our worth, like attracts like. Once we are conscious enough, before we reincarnate we work out the country, the parents, the physical condition, the circumstances and the experiences of our Earth lives according to the lessons we wish to learn. We are of course helped and advised by others around us. There is always help on request.

I loved my parents and they were both loving people, but not demonstratively so. I can never remember either of them being angry with me but it has to be said that there was hardly any emotion of any kind in the house. My father never sat me on his knee and I don't remember either of them ever raising their voices. I think it was part of the times but it has left a lasting impression – to this day it upsets me to hear raised voices. Mother and Father always seemed very happy together: they both played golf and enjoyed bridge parties. One of my most comfortable childhood memories is of sitting on the stairs with my sister, listening to visitors downstairs playing bridge and having a few drinks.

My sister and I got on well, though we didn't have a lot in common. She had her own friends and in general she would do her own thing and leave me to get on with mine.

Sometimes, though, she would take advantage of the fact that I was three years younger. To reach our bedrooms we had to cross a long dark corridor connecting the bathroom, which was in the old cottage, to the main house. Beryl would always dare me to go down the corridor on my own and switch the bathroom light on. 'You're frightened, aren't you?' she would taunt. I would always fall for it and race down the corridor, just to prove I wasn't scared at all. It took a while before I realized that Beryl was just as frightened as I was.

She would also love to set me off giggling. Almost anything would make me dissolve into fits of giggles, often at the most inopportune moment. I just seemed to have an over-developed sense of the ridiculous. At Rutland House the doorbell rang all day long with people coming to pick up their prescriptions and Beryl and I would take turns to answer it. When it was my turn, she would stand behind a curtain in the hall and make a sniggering sound. That would be all too much and I would find it almost impossible to keep a straight face, even when the caller was telling me about some terrible illness.

Eventually my father gave us a warning about this, as it was hardly benefiting his patients. That very evening I answered the door. A man stood there.

'Good evening,' I said carefully.

'Good evening,' he replied. 'Could I see the doctor, please?'

'Who shall I say is calling?'

'Mr Onions.'

That was it. I burst out laughing right in his face. Leaving him on the doorstep, I staggered into the drawing room and literally collapsed with laughter.

After a while, I managed to actually ask Beryl if she would tell our father there was someone at the door. Seeing the state I was in, she couldn't resist telling me to go myself.

Trying hard to compose myself, I knocked on the surgery door.

'Come in.' My father had a patient with him. They both turned to look at me.

'There's ... there's a Mr...' No, I couldn't do it. I reeled out of the surgery, howling with laughter.

Beryl and I got the biggest ticking-off of

our lives for that one. But it still didn't cure me of giggling.

When I was four-and-a-half years old, my mother took me to a nearby terraced house, Chilwel House, in Lord Haddon Road. Its front room was actually a school.

I really only remember my first day there. When we walked in, accompanied by the teacher, we saw two wooden desks with benches attached. Seven or eight children were crawling underneath them on the floor. They paid no attention to us at all. Eventually the teacher managed to make a small speech welcoming me to the school, but I didn't stay there long. I soon moved on to the Steiner school next door to Rutland House.

It was Steiner's philosophy that children should be educated in a free and loving environment full of music, dancing and painting, and formal education should not be imposed on them until they were ten years old. It was my great fortune to enjoy all this for two-and-a-half years at Michael House School.

What we learned more than anything else was to care for other people and take responsibility for our own actions. Strangely, discipline was not needed, as it seemed out of place to misbehave. There was a feeling of harmony which no one wanted to disrupt, and there was kindness and patience from the teachers, which dissolved all aggression. It was a very memorable and colourful experience, and no doubt helped to nurture the seeds that would later flower into spiritual awareness.

'You get back what you give out in thought, word and deed.'

It was also at Michael House that I appeared on stage for the first time. It was as a tree. I think it was an oak. A non-speaking role. The play was one of the school's regular theatrical performances and I had to stand in the background with my arms outstretched. This soon became agony and I decided to support myself by surreptitiously holding on to the curtains behind me. This move brought the house down – or more literally the curtains – and that was the end of the show.

My mother, who was herself a keen amateur actress, was quite angry with me, not for bringing down the curtains but for spoiling my own performance. So I learned that it didn't matter if you ruined the whole

production as long as your own performance was good! A valuable lesson for the
future, as it turned out.

CHAPTER 2

School and War

*'It is not possible to have an earthly existence
freed from problems, difficulties or troubles,
because that is why you are born
into your world.'*

I was seven years old when the Second World
War began. I remember clearly sitting in the
drawing room at Rutland House with my
family listening to the declaration of war with
Germany. At the time I had no idea how it
had started and whether it was morally right
or wrong; I just knew how it affected us.

The main thing was that food was rationed
and sweets were rare. I didn't see a shop full
of sweets on general sale until I was 14.
Sometimes even now I get a sense of excitement when I see a shop window or a coun-
ter full of sweets and chocolates, and can

hardly believe that I can actually buy as many as I want.

The two wrought-iron gates at the end of our drive were taken away as part of the war effort. I remember the feeling of sadness when they were taken down. They were never replaced.

Our garden was given over to flocks of ducks and hens. They wandered everywhere, including down the now gateless drive and onto the road. They didn't have any proper nesting boxes, so one of my jobs was to hunt for the nests and collect the eggs.

All the windows of the house had to be covered with heavy curtains or blinds as part of the blackout precautions. At night everything was blacked out and you couldn't show a light. We were also issued with gas masks, which we had to carry in cardboard boxes hung round our necks with string.

Everyone had to have an air-raid shelter or a safe room in the house. We didn't have a shelter and our safe room was the kitchen. This was at the back of the house. It had just one window and had rooms on the other three sides, so it was fairly well protected. We put steel shutters over the window and whenever the air-raid warning went off we all went and sat there. Of course, if there had been a direct hit, you would be a goner, no question. But it was warm and cosy sitting round the fire drinking Ovaltine and listening to the radio, and I never really felt threatened by the war. The only thing was, my sister told me that if you walked on the cracks on the pavement the Germans would come. I avoided the cracks.

Not long after the war began I was sent away to boarding school. After the relaxed atmosphere and creativity at Michael House, this was something of a shock.

At that time my cousin Harry was at Rydal School in Colwyn Bay, North Wales, and his sister Audrey was at Penrhos, a girls' school in the same town. Because of this connection, and the fact that the area was fairly remote and free of bombing, my parents decided I should go to Rydal too and Beryl to Penrhos.

When I arrived the senior school buildings had been requisitioned by the Ministry of Food and the senior school had been evacuated to Oakwood Park in Conway. So there was just the junior school there at the time, at Beech House, a very big house set in a large garden.

I arrived there with my parents after dropping Beryl off at Penrhos the previous day. Beech House seemed an impressive place. An imposing front door opened into a hall as big as a ballroom. Its centrepiece was a striking oak staircase.

My parents took me in and Matron, a pleasant woman of indeterminate age, met us. She was in uniform, a simple blue dress with white starched cuffs and collar and a white apron. She took us up the staircase to a dormitory which had six unsprung iron beds in it. On one of them was a dark blue tartan rug that I recognized from home, and that was my bed for the next year.

Watching from the window as my parents got into the car and drove away, I felt rather lonely and frightened. But soon more boys arrived and I noticed that the new arrivals were all well looked after. We were each allocated a senior boy who was to look after us. Mine was called John Howarth. That first day he arrived back at the school with his father, Jack Howarth, a small round man who ran the repertory company in Colwyn Bay. He carried an ivory-topped cane, which I thought was very impressive.

He asked my name and where I came from. Where *did* I come from? After some thought, I said, 'England.'

Jack thought that was very amusing and he reminded me of it 20 years later when I met him again, when he was playing Ken's Uncle Albert in *Coronation Street*.

I was a little frightened at first. The bed was hard and it was strange to be living in a new place with so many people. But Matron, known as 'Tronna', was not unkind and she became the centre of our lives. We turned to her for everything during that first year. It was quite a wrench in the second year when another batch of new boys arrived and we had to start coping without her.

'As you strive with others, so your own brightness increases.'

Some things were difficult to get used to, of course, most notably the cold baths. Every morning in the summer we would stand stark naked in a line in front of a bath filled with cold water and each of us in turn would jump in. Tronna, sitting in a chair by the bath, would not let us get out until we had completely submerged ourselves. She would then hand us a towel and we would run back over the cold linoleum to the dorm. If it was supposed to be character building, it didn't work with me – to this day I cannot stand cold draughty houses and keep the central heating on all year round.

I found I could get along easily with the other boys and throughout junior school I even had a nickname. This came courtesy of Mr Lewis, the junior school headmaster, who remarked one evening, 'Do you know that a roache is a fish? I think Roache should be called Fish, don't you?' Fortunately that was dropped when I moved on to the senior school.

Michael House had been an inspiring place, but the focus had not been on academic work and I found that I was way behind all the other boys in the basic subjects. I was also left-handed, which was regarded as an abnormality by our form teacher, Miss Corbett. She was a straightforward, no-nonsense, jolly-hockey-sticks type and whenever I wrote with my left hand she applied 'remedial treatment' by hitting me across the knuckles with a ruler. Reluctantly, I had to start writing with my right. Apart from appalling writing, this caused some interesting effects such as writing letters back to front. Nowadays it would probably be called a form of dyslexia. It became so bad that on being asked to write an essay on dogs, I wrote 'god' all the way through. Should have made interesting reading.

I also started to stammer a little, and in this I was in good company, as the stammer of King George VI is usually attributed to the attempts to make him right-handed. At this point the remedial treatment was stopped and I was allowed to carry on using my left hand. Soon afterwards the dyslexia and the stammering fell away.

Another problem, and rather an embarrassing one, was my persistent bedwetting. This had been going on for some time and got worse at Beech House, if anything. It was terribly shaming, because if the bed was wet, it would be stripped and the mattress put out to air where everyone could see it. Every morning I would lie there, afraid to move in case I encountered a wet patch.

The only comfort was that I wasn't alone in this. There were four of us and we were all put together in one dormitory. Fortunately, we were all good at sport and well liked, so were protected somewhat from the humiliation normally inflicted on bedwetters.

The school did its best to cure us of our problem. We weren't allowed to drink after teatime and were woken in the night to go to the loo. When this didn't work, Mr Lewis, the junior school headmaster, decided not to let us sleep on our backs, as he had read that bedwetting only occurred when you were on your back. Pa Louie, as he was known, had harnesses made of white fabric tape with cotton reels threaded along it. The idea was that we would sleep wrapped in this tape and if we rolled onto our backs the cotton reels would dig in and wake us up. But morning after morning we would be found, having shrugged these Heath Robinson contraptions off in our sleep, flat on our backs in a wet patch. Within a week this plan was abandoned as well.

Fortunately, we all grew out of bedwetting in time. I was around ten when it finally stopped.

Now I know that it's only by overcoming some form of suffering, some problem, that we get the strength and the wisdom to move forward. And so we have all set ourselves tasks to overcome. It is very hard to accept that all the difficulties and suffering we encounter were planned. And, what is more, planned by us, with a little help from higher beings. But they are necessary for our spiritual unfolding. So we should always welcome our difficulties as opportunities and remember that we are never given more than we can stand. I believe the problems I had at school did strengthen me in some way.

One of the things that being sent to boarding school did was lead me to be able to look after myself wherever I went. I still like to make my own little area wherever I go, my own little nest. Although it also taught me to get on with people, I sought out private places where I could be alone and this included an abandoned house that I broke into and turned into my secret hideaway – secret, that is, until an estate agent turned up with a prospective buyer and I had to hide in a cupboard.

Sport was a part of this too. I played cricket a lot at school. I was an opening batsman, batting right-handed for some reason. I was a steady bat. I could stay in, but if ever runs were needed quickly, I wasn't the man. I'd lose my concentration and be out. I found that games could teach you a lot about yourself. And about other people. I was also a slow left-arm bowler, and if ever anybody had dug themselves in, I'd be brought on to bowl a couple of overs. I'd probably be hit for six and hit for four and then the batsman would be out, because they would get too relaxed with someone like me bowling. That was another lesson. I was never a killer player in any way, but I used to enjoy it.

I also liked rugby. I played for the school at both rugby and cricket. In rugby I played scrum half, which is where you get jumped on by all the heavy forwards and bear the brunt of it all. I'm not sure what that says about me!

Once after a cricket match against the naval college side from HMS *Conway* we were taken on board the old ship for tea and before we left a bugler sounded the Last Post. It moved me very much and it was almost as if it brought back a memory of a previous life. At the time I didn't think it through, but this feeling has stayed with me and all my life I have been tremendously excited by the sound of a trumpet or bugle.

Outside our little world at school the war was going on, but it was all strangely remote. My father would have been just coming up to 40 when it started and he wasn't called up. Certain doctors stayed behind and he was one of them. He ran Ilkeston Hospital and worked with the local Air Raid Precaution group. So I never had the sense that there was someone close to me involved in the fighting. Uncle John spent the whole of the war in Gibraltar, in the Royal Army Medical Corps, so he didn't have any particularly hair-raising stories to tell when he came home on leave. And I never saw wounded soldiers returning home. I had a protected war, really, in the sense of brutality and cruelty and carnage – there was nothing of that. My fear of death didn't start with the war.

In a way it was almost like a game. I remember in the drawing room at Rutland House we had a big map of North Africa and the Mediterranean on the wall, and it had little flags stuck into it. My father used to listen to the radio and move the flags along according to where the British forces were and what was happening. It was fascinating to see him doing this. I remember him being quite upbeat and I think this must have been towards the end of the North African campaign when we were pushing Rommel back and Montgomery was leading the assault. Moving the flags forward just seemed like a fun thing to do. I never actually made the connection with armies slaughtering each other.

Generally speaking, I didn't think about what was happening much at all. Provided my day unfolded as it should, everything was fine. I had no inclination to think beyond that. I don't know if I should have. Some children are very enquiring, full of curiosity about the world, but I wasn't – not then, anyway.

At school, we were well fed, considering the times, and were even allowed four pieces of special blended chocolate on a Saturday afternoon. I didn't in any way feel deprived, although I would sometimes fantasize that my desk was full of sweets and bars of chocolate.

Rationed food was kept in a second-floor room at Beech House and no one was allowed up there. Occasionally, though, we would gang together, post a lookout and take it in turns to help ourselves to a lump of sugar or some dried fruit. We never took much and it was as much for the thrill of being naughty as anything else.

Then one Saturday afternoon a full house assembly was called in the billiards room. This was a rare event and we expected an important announcement. When all 40 of us were in our seats, Mr Lewis arrived, looking grim.

'I am horrified and appalled,' he announced. 'There is a thief in the school. Someone has been into the food store and stolen a box of raisins.'

We all sat in guilty silence. I was blushing furiously. 'If he looks at me,' I thought, 'he'll think I did it.'

'I will give the boy responsible the chance to do the honourable thing and own up,' Mr Lewis continued.

No one moved.

'Very well,' Mr Lewis said. 'I am going up to my study. You will all remain here until the culprit comes to me and admits his guilt.' He left the room.

We sat in silence for a long while. Eventually someone whispered, 'Does anyone know who did it?' No one answered. The clock ticked by. Our Saturday afternoons were our own and we usually spent them out in the gardens, not shut up in the billiard room. At one point a boy offered to own up just to get us out of there, but in the end he changed his mind.

After two agonizing hours Mr Lewis finally came back and let us go, but he told us that we would all have to reassemble in the billiard room every day after lunch until the thief owned up.

I was firmly convinced I'd be spending half my life there, but the very next morning we learned who the culprit was. It seemed he had not only taken the box of raisins but eaten them all as well. This had been too much for his bowels to cope with and during the night the fatal evidence had appeared in his bed. Mr Lewis caned him for theft.

Apart from the rationing, our other main reminder of the war was seeing evacuees arriving in Colwyn Bay. These were children from London and other big towns who were being moved to safer areas. We watched them being distributed to people, clutching their suitcases and gas masks in cardboard boxes. This was something I never saw at home because we were too near to Derby to be regarded as a safe area. Evacuees were always sent to outlying areas like North Wales.

Some of these 'vacees' would come round the school wall and we regarded them as a sort of yobbo element. I know we should have had great sympathy for these poor kids away from their home, but no, they were an enemy. Whenever we saw them we'd call out, *'Vacees!* Over at the wall!' and then we'd all go out and shout things at them. They'd shout back, too. Somebody threw something at somebody once. That was as far as it went, though.

Then one day when we were playing football we saw a German fighter flying over the field. The game stopped as we all stared up at it. We could see it quite clearly. It was black, with a swastika underneath. The pilot was obviously trying to escape from somewhere and get back home, and he just flew low across us and away. I've no idea what happened to him.

My sister's school, however, was actually machine-gunned. Penrhos had been evacuated to Chatsworth House in Derbyshire, and that's where it happened. The classrooms were machine-gunned by a German plane that went by, but fortunately everyone was in the school chapel at the time and no one was hurt. Divine Providence! That brought the reality of the war home to my sister.

I was more interested in the military hardware. We never had any bombs where we were in Ilkeston, though a couple landed not far away. But Derby, ten miles away, where the Rolls-Royce works were, was bombed a lot. Every time I was taken to school or picked up on the way back, I had to go to Derby railway station and we always passed a barrage balloon. These were big grey balloons sent up at night to stop planes. They were shaped like Zeppelins with little fins on. The great steel cable that took each balloon up to a great height would get in the way of planes coming in at a low angle and would cut their wings off and bring them down. During the day the barrage balloons themselves were pulled down. Whenever I was driven past the one at Derby I would gaze at it, absolutely fascinated.

Each barrage balloon also had big search-lights beside it and I was intrigued by how they worked, by the mechanics of it all, but I didn't really think about what they were there for. When you're young you tend not to think much beyond your own environment, and I didn't, even though there was a war going on.

One thing that did strike me was seeing a rifle propped up in the kitchen at Rutland House. It belonged to the boyfriend of one of the maids, Alice. She was a very jolly and pleasant person and I used to spend a lot of time with her. I looked at the rifle and thought, 'That looks quite exciting.' But again, it didn't really hit home to me what it was for.

*'Whilst there are slaughterhouses,
there will be battlefields.'*

In many ways my childhood was very free and casual. When I was on holiday I'd just go off on my bike, and I'd be away all day, down by the canal or off in the countryside, and nobody ever bothered as long as I was home for mealtimes. Otherwise I was free to do whatever I wanted.

I was also free to find things out for myself. My parents didn't feel they had to take me off to evening classes or that I had to join the scouts or the cubs or any of that. I was left to do my own thing, and I did. I used to spend a lot of time building dens in the garden. I loved making things out of wood.

I tended to be on my own quite a lot. The trouble with boarding school is that you don't see your friends in the holidays and you don't tend to have friends in your local area. There were a couple of boys I used to play with in the early days, but they gradually moved away, so the holidays were generally spent pushing about on my own – which I liked. I didn't feel lonely. On the contrary, I was very happy to be on my own. In many ways it was a welcome contrast to school. It was nice to get home and sit around and just set my own agenda and do my own thing.

One summer evening I was listening to an Al Jolson record on our wind-up gramophone and the needle needed changing. When I went to get a replacement, I found a little tin full of old needles. Without thinking, I threw them out of the window. To my horror, they were immediately gobbled up by a flock of greedy hens. Feeling pretty guilty, I watched the hens closely over the next few days, but remarkably there didn't seem to be any ill effects.

Life wasn't always that easy for my family, however. While I was away at school my mother's father, Albert, committed suicide at Rutland House. He cut his throat with a razor and took two days to die. My father looked after him but in all that time my mother never saw him. At the time I was unaware of all the details, but I remember receiving a letter from my mother telling me that Grandpa had died. I felt sad and cried. He had always been there and now he was gone. Uncle John meanwhile was doing surprisingly well in the army. He had actually worked his way up through the ranks to become a quartermaster. The family put this down to the fact that there was a war on. He continued to visit us whenever he was on leave, leaving a trail of empty bottles behind him and quietly purloining small household items like soap and toothpaste. I was later told that he tried to seduce my mother on one occasion and did succeed in seducing a 14-year-old cousin of mine who was staying in the house. The final straw, however, came when my father watched him stealing money from his wallet. After that, his visits were restricted.

Back at school I was finding out more about the world around me. On Sunday afternoons we would go for a walk in 'crocodile'. That was being paired off in twos forming a long line. 'Croc up!' would go the cry, and we would all fall in and set off on the walk. You could only really talk to the boy you were paired with and it was on one of these walks that I received my sex education. I had a bit of a problem understanding the mechanics, but basically what my companion told me was accurate – apart from that if your mother was limping in the morning it was because she had 'done it' the night before!

My parents never told me anything about sex and there was no instruction from the teachers in those days, so that Sunday afternoon walk was my one and only sex lesson – from another ten-year-old. It seems remarkable now, but that's what it was like in those days. Whereas now there's everything at school – information, counselling even – then it was up to you to find things out for yourself

Around the age of nine or ten most of us had found out about masturbation. It was looked on as a sort of hobby more than anything else and has become associated in my mind with an 'official' hobby that was a school craze at the time – collecting chewing gum and chocolate wrappers dropped by the American GIs stationed nearby. Whenever we would see a GI we would call out, 'Got any gum, chum?', but we actually wanted the wrappers as much as the gum itself. We would stick them in scrapbooks and build up whole collections. The whole school went mad on it.

One day a boy found a square packet that no one had seen before. We gathered round to look at this strange new chewing gum. It was called Durex.

CHAPTER 3

'All That's Left of the School Dramatic Society...'

*'There are more things in Heaven and
Earth, Horatio, than are dreamt of
in your philosophy.'*
Hamlet, I, v, 166–7

Time moved on and I began the hormonally charged years of puberty. I don't know if there was any connection, but it was then that I had two psychic experiences.

The first one happened in the bathroom at Rutland House, a long thin room about 10 foot long, with the loo at the back facing the door. It was while I was sitting on the loo – a good place to be for what happened subsequently – that I suddenly looked towards the door and there it was.

It was an ill-defined shape standing in the doorway. The outline was that of someone with a sheet thrown over them, but it was all a gritty grey colour and staring out of it was a pair of yellow eyes. They were looking right at me.

Literally frozen with fear, I looked down, desperately trying to think what to do. There was no escape – it was in the doorway.

When I finally forced myself to look back, it had gone.

I had no idea what it was. There was no question of a trick of the light. It was broad daylight and quite a clear day.

I never told anyone about this incident, but now I knew why my sister used to make me run to the bathroom to switch on the light. She always felt that there was something down there and she was afraid of it.

For a while I was very wary of going down that corridor, but whatever it was, I never saw it again.

Since then I have heard that water is an energy field that can be used by discarnate beings to manifest in the material world, and I have wondered about the old well that was just under the bathroom. During the war it was part of the emergency water supply, so obviously water ran in there somehow or other, maybe from a spring.

I was shaken by the experience, but gradually I got over it. After that, whenever people talked about ghosts or paranormal phenomena I would think back to that shape, but it didn't set me off enquiring, which is what these things are meant to do. I would want to know about anything strange, to hear all the details, but I would leave it there. I didn't start enquiring seriously into such matters until years later.

The other paranormal experience I had was very different. Again I was at home. One night I woke suddenly to find bright moonlight shining into my room, making it almost like daylight, and there, floating just above the foot of my bed, was a large light-blue Buddha. With it came a beautiful feeling of peace. Although I am not a Buddhist, I do feel an affinity with Buddhism and possibly it was something I embraced in a previous life. Again, I never told anyone about this experience. I didn't really know how to explain it, or what to say, so I just kept it to myself.

It was around this time that I was having the very unpleasant experience of waking up in the morning unable to move. Only after a superhuman effort could I suddenly break free of this, and I would dread going to sleep knowing what was waiting for me when I awoke.

I did ask people about this inability to move in the morning, but no one seemed to understand it. My father dismissed it with, 'It will pass.' Later on, through my metaphysical studies, I found the explanation. At night, while we sleep, our spirits leave our bodies and go onto another plane, the astral plane, and actively participate in the life there. Sometimes we can wake up before our astral bodies have fully returned, and this was what was happening to me. Fortunately, after a short time, it stopped. Perhaps I had just started visiting the astral plane and was taking a while to adjust to the experience.

Let me explain: when a spiritual being is ready and wants to incarnate, it isn't just a bit of pure spirit suddenly plunged into a physical body; there's a gradual descent through lower and lower vibrations. So imagine a bit of pure spirit which has to descend into something like a big heavy diving suit at the bottom of the sea, and that is our physical body. Our physical body is just a vehicle in which we can function on the material plane. The spirit lowers its vibrations gradually, starting with what we call the mental body, which is a slightly lower vibrational shell. Then it descends into an even lower vibration, which is the desire body getting an even thicker shell on it before descending into an etheric body. The etheric body is the lowest vibration before the physical body of which it is an exact replica. In it are all the plans for the type of being it is going to become and to some extent its destiny – just like an oak tree is inside an acorn. This is planted into the embryo and the vehicle for the incarnation begins to grow. The incarnating spiritual being is around during the conception and makes the final descent into the embryo, sealing off all memory within the first three months. Science has proved some of this in a way by the discovery of DNA, which gives an indication of your physical destiny, appearance and, quite often, how you are going to go out of this world. This would be shown by you being predisposed to a disease. Sceptics will ask, 'Well, what if a cure is discovered for your predisposed disease?' The answer to that is, 'If a cure is discovered while you are here, that is part of your karma, it is not by chance. There are no accidents in God's world, so by and large our destiny is laid out – but we do have free will.'

Now the people who are in contact on this side have an affinity with someone in the spiritual realms and can communicate with great clarity. This is done either telepathically by automatic writing or by actually using a medium. Either method will describe in detail what the spiritual realms are like. The philosophy of Silver Birch – a native American Indian who was a great teacher – was communicated through a medium called Maurice Barbanell. Barbanell would hold meetings at which Silver Birch would convey through him words of such outstanding wisdom that they were written down and, happily, these books can be bought and read to this day.

Some people work consciously on the astral plane. Rudolf Steiner was apparently able to have meetings there with people who were physically far away and he was able to remember clearly all that happened.

When we sleep we visit the astral plane and when we return we have no recollection of this because it is our mind that has gone out and not our brain. However, there is an exercise for developing the ability to remember more of these astral visits. As you are slipping into sleep, try to keep your consciousness with you. After a while you will find that you are able to do this for longer and longer periods. Also make the effort to actively participate in your dreams – try to have some say in what is going on. Instead of your dream being something you are looking at, you are there in it, so involve yourself – you can. Learning to participate in your dreams can bring you useful insights into your life and help you to move forward.

I knew nothing of this during my teenage years, but it was at this time that I started trying to find out more about what everything meant. I knew there were answers out there somewhere, but where?

I was driven by two great fears, both of which really emerged during adolescence. The first was the fear of death. I was so frightened of it that I could not talk about it. Just to see the word would trigger the fear. I couldn't believe that something as sophisticated as a human being could just end.

This fear was especially acute when my father had to go out and visit people with an infectious disease. I was always terrified that he would bring it back. This went on for years. I was particularly frightened during the big polio epidemic of 1949. This was in the days before the vaccine was discovered. It is amazing in fact how rarely doctors contract a disease like this from their patients. It's probably because their immune systems are so tough. But their bravery is taken for granted.

Generally my father never discussed his patients, though I remember him once talking about going out to see a miner who had his whole leg ripped off, right up to the groin, in some machinery. He had died of his injury. But that was really the only time I remember my father speaking about the people he had treated.

I myself didn't have any serious illnesses during my childhood. I was very fortunate. I didn't have anything, apart from measles, and that very mildly. I remember the whole school went down with chicken pox once and there were only four of us who didn't get it and we were put in the isolation ward. My sister was pretty healthy too. I think I remember her having mumps at one point, but that was all.

The closest I had come to death in any form was when I was about 12 or 13 and was home for the summer holidays.

At that time my Great Aunt Ede was living with us in the room next to mine. She was small and thin and smoked like a chimney all day long and drank Wincarnis fortified wine. She was always asking me to get a bottle for her – I didn't mind as I was very fond of her.

Then one morning my mother came in with a cup of tea for me, which was unheard of, and she said, 'Auntie Ede has died.' As she went back downstairs, I realized the tea had been meant for my aunt.

While I was getting dressed, I kept thinking, 'In the next room, my aunt is lying dead.' I'd never seen anyone dead. So I made myself go in and have a look.

It was something of an anticlimax. Auntie Ede was lying there quite peacefully and to my surprise I didn't feel anything particularly. As I stood there looking at her, my only thought was, 'I wonder if you've got any sweet coupons left,' which, I know, was dreadful.

As far as I was concerned Auntie Ede had just gone. I didn't think about where she'd gone. Even though I was afraid of death, when I saw her lying there like that, all I felt was the realization that she wouldn't be there any more. I did say goodbye, but that was all. I didn't think beyond that.

Death was still frightening, and now more immediate. A little later on I suddenly started to get palpitations. It was probably just an adolescent hormonal thing, but I was convinced there was something seriously wrong with me and I was going to die. I walked around very carefully for a couple of days, just in case any sudden movement finished me off, and finally I thought I'd better tell my father.

I waited until he'd finished surgery then knocked on the door.

He said, 'Yes, come in.'

This time I was very polite and formal in my father's surgery. Besides, it was hardly a giggling matter. I said simply, 'I think I've got something wrong with me.'

He said, 'What's the matter?'

I said 'It's my heart. It's palpitating. I think it's quite serious.'

'Come here,' was his response.

I walked cautiously towards him and to my horror, he reached out and pushed me, punched me almost, in the chest. I crashed backwards into the wall, thinking, *My God! You've killed me!*

'Look,' said my father, 'I've got enough all day with people being ill. I don't want you coming in at the end of surgery adding to my problems.'

I stared at him in amazement then got up and walked out, thinking, *Great! A doctor who doesn't care about his own family!*

I felt quite indignant for a while and then as I calmed down I suddenly realized that I felt all right. I wasn't going to die after all. And from that moment the palpitations disappeared.

I don't know how my father knew it wasn't

anything serious. He was not a violent man and that single punch – more of a hefty shove, really – was the only time he ever laid hands on me. He had probably seen me walking around carefully thinking I might die on the spot. But what he did was totally right – it snapped me out of it and I didn't have to go knocking on the surgery door again.

My other great fear was also one which led me to look into esoteric philosophy. This was just as strong as my fear of death and may at first seem strange. But sometimes I would look up at the stars and think of a spaceship with self-generating fuel setting off in a straight line. I would imagine it going on and on, and on and on, and on and on and on and on and on... Then there would come a point when my brain felt that it was going to explode and I would have what we now call a panic attack. I was terrified by infinity.

The thing was, there was something different out there, something beyond our comprehension. We were incapable of understanding it. Why?

I wanted to know more. I needed to know more. No one had taught us about anything like that at school and my parents hadn't either. It was particularly unnerving to think that there was this conspiracy of silence. Something inside me said, *There is some information here that I'm not getting.* I wanted to get it.

I didn't know where to turn. I tried the Church. We weren't great churchgoers in our family and I had never been sent to Sunday school or anything like that. My father was quite friendly with the local vicar, but that was a social thing – doctors, vicars and MPs were respected members of society and they got together. Reverend Butterton was a nice old guy, but we'd only go to church, other than for weddings, funerals and so on, about once or twice a year. So I asked the school chaplain instead. But he wouldn't answer my questions and neither would the headmaster. I even had arguments with them over it. That started quite early on, when I was around 11 or so.

At home there weren't any answers either. My sister and I never discussed anything significant. We weren't particularly close at that age. I was always very much the little boy, the junior. So I couldn't get any information from her.

Strangely, I didn't blame my parents for not telling me whatever it was. I didn't think they even knew, because they would have told me if they had. It didn't seem to me that such questions bothered them that much. My father was simply getting on with keeping people alive and my mother was a wonderful hard-working mother.

Soon I realized that the grown-ups I looked to for answers couldn't tell me what I wanted to know. It ought to have been part of my education, but it wasn't. And no one else was even asking these sort of questions. I felt totally alone.

This wasn't as bad as it may sound, however, as in those days it was the norm to have to find your own way. You were left to find out quite important things for yourself. Nowadays of course everybody talks about everything all the time – you see people opening up their hearts on television every day – but back then you had the feeling that it was up to you to find the answers to any questions you had.

It was similar if you had a problem of any kind – you didn't go to counsellors, you just had to sort yourself out. I'm not saying it was good or bad, and in fact it was lonely in many ways, but the idea was that keeping a stiff upper lip was good for you. It was quite a tough attitude, but was pretty much the attitude of the day. And people will be born into a certain era because it's right for them, so in some way or other that was right for me. I think that growing up during the Second World War did make me self-reliant, so at some level I must have needed that. Certainly I didn't feel in any way deprived or badly treated because no one had the answers I craved. That was just the way it was.

Now, looking back, I am certain that my two great fears were deliberately given to me, and I can see the purpose behind them. It was the fear of death that led me to find out what happens after death and it was the fear of infinity that made me look beyond the material world. So I thank my higher self for giving me those fears, because they led me to search for understanding. They set me on the right path.

So I would say look at your fears, because overcoming those fears, or even simply facing them, is something that's going to help you. There's always something good in your fears. They're not very nice – in fact they're horrible – but if you can overcome them, you will have taken a great step forward. It may be that you don't even need to overcome them but just to look at them and see where they might lead you. Realize that fear is there for a reason. It will give you a greater understanding of yourself. All fears can be overcome.

One fear I had to face up to was moving on to the senior school at Oakwood Park. But once I was there, I soon got used to it. It had a very different atmosphere from the junior school, but we all had a lot more freedom there.

Oakwood Park had been a hotel and golf course before the war and was in a beautiful setting facing Conway Mountain. I spent two years there before returning to the main building back at Colwyn Bay to complete my education. My classroom was in the former cocktail bar and overlooked a large lawn. I remember spending most of my time looking out of the window.

One day it was particularly interesting, as a small herd of Welsh ponies arrived on the lawn and stood around grazing while a mare started foaling. In a very short time the foal was born and within minutes the mother was pushing it with her nose, trying to get it to stand on its gangly legs. Eventually she succeeded and it was heart-warming to watch her gently nosing it as it wobbled about as though on stilts. Soon the herd set off again, the long-legged foal lunging and lurching at its mother's side, and I marvelled at how the herd instinctively knew when the foal was able to keep up with it. The whole process had taken under two hours. I learned a lot in the classroom that day, but not from the teachers.

Though we had a lot more free time at the senior school, on Monday evenings between the hours of six and eight it was compulsory to pursue a hobby. There was a wide variety to choose from, but they all seemed to demand a lot of mental or physical energy. I stood with my friend Tuckey in front of a notice board displaying all the options and we struggled to find something that was not too exacting.

Behind us the door to the school hall was open, revealing a small group of boys lounging about on the back seats. Some had their feet over the seat in front of them, one was reading a comic and another was yawning. Without a word, Tuckey and I started walking towards them.

As we joined the loungers, we became aware of a small group of senior boys at the other end of the hall having an altercation with a master. We could not hear what was being said, but suddenly all the senior boys turned and left the hall. The master paused for a moment, looked at us, and then, as he slowly walked towards us, said, 'I am afraid that you are all that's left of the school dramatic society.'

That's how my acting life began. At least that's how I remember it but in hindsight I think that Tuckey had already decided and took me with him. He went on to become a very successful theatre director.

It would be good to say there had been a strong vocational calling to do drama. There hadn't, not at that point. But I do know that nothing happens by accident and that there is no such thing as a coincidence. It was meant to be.

My friend and I went on to become the leading lights of the society, both of us in turn winning the drama prize, in my case when I appeared in Ibsen's *Enemy of the People*. However, for the first few years I was given all the female parts, including Lady M. in Shakespeare's unmentionable.

My mother came up to see me in this. She was a keen amateur actress and directed all the plays for the Townswomen's Guild of Ilkeston. This was the first time she had managed to see me in anything since the curtain incident and I was eager to please her. I got through the performance without grinding to a halt and afterwards I was expecting a few nice comments, but instead, without any preamble, she started to give me notes on how I could improve my performance. I can't even remember what they were, as I was too busy thinking she could have said, 'Well done, but...' However, she did mean well and her notes were no doubt a big contributing factor to my eventual success in the school dramatic society.

'Expectation and desire are bride and bridegroom.'

Not everything went well, however. Music was important to me, but I was bad at it. I wanted to be able to sing and I couldn't. There was a school choir – in fact there was a concert choir with Penrhos that did the *Messiah* – but I would never have got in it. This was really my first experience of wanting to be good at something but not making it. I dreamed about being able to get up and sing, but I could never hold a tune properly.

Instead I took up the piano, then, after a year, transferred to the trumpet. I desperately wanted to be a really good trumpet player and I practised away and practised away. In vain. The neighbours in Ilkeston always knew when I was home – they'd hear an awful trumpet noise blasting out of the back room. I was never any good.

I did, however, have the distinction of being the only trumpet player in the school. In fact I was a kind of oddball because I was the only one. I desperately wanted to play with other people and sadly there wasn't a school band or orchestra. Once I even went and asked my father if I could join the Salvation Army, because they were the only band in the area, and he said that wasn't the right reason for joining, which was quite right, so that was it. Nevertheless, in the school music competition, which took place every year, I used to play something accompanied on the piano. I did 'Jerusalem' once wearing my rugby blazer and the adjudicator said he thought I should stick to rugby and forget the trumpet.

Taking up the trumpet, what does that tell you? A single instrument blasting out – you can't get more individualistic than that! I was beginning to want to stand out in some way.

I started to have a go at anything that excited or interested me, even – or especially – if I couldn't do it. I'm still like that – if there's something I think I can't do, I will try to do it all the same.

Back when I was about 17 or 18, I desperately wanted a car and our maid Renée's husband Sam had just bought one. I can't even remember the make of it now, but it was a strange contraption mainly made out of wood. I'd just got my driving licence and I went with Sam to Newstead Abbey, Byron's former home, to collect it and drove him back. It wasn't far, 15 miles maybe, and in those days there wasn't so much traffic on the road, but I never thought about insurance, tax or anything like that, and it was quite a difficult car to drive. It was amazing that Sam let me do it, really, but I did have a great rapport with Sam and Renée. Their daughter, Janet, still writes to me occasionally – it's been a great friendship.

Roughly around the same time that I drove the car for the first time, a friend of mine had a motorbike.

'I'm leaving it at school during the holidays,' he told me.

'Oh, it's a really nice bike,' I said wistfully.

'Well, you can borrow it if you want.'

I hadn't got tax, insurance or a licence. I said, 'Oh, yes.'

'Can you ride a motorbike?'

'Yeah.'

I'd never ridden a motorbike in my life and this was a BSA 250cc, quite a powerful bike. I don't know why my parents let me do it or what I'd told them I was doing. I just might have said I was bringing it on the train...

Anyway, I set off optimistically from Colwyn Bay, wearing goggles and a leather helmet like a Japanese kamikaze pilot, and stayed in first gear for the first 20 miles because I didn't know how to change gear.

By the time I reached Snake Pass there was a snowstorm. I was only wearing a light raincoat and the snow kept building up on my goggles. Finally, I got a nosebleed and had to stop. I pulled in at the Cat and Fiddle.

As I stumbled through the door, all snow and blood, the barman said, 'We're closed.'

'I'm a traveller in distress!'

'We're still closed.'

I stormed back out and the annoyance from that encounter – I was tempted to write anger there but I don't get angry and I don't like to see it in others – got me going and I carried right on to Ilkeston. I can't remember how long it took me. I fell off twice, skidding in the snow. But I could ride a motorbike when I got home.

I was actually quite ill by then and had to

stay in bed for two days. But I'd done it.

That's what I was like then – if there was something I really wanted, I wouldn't think about the consequences or the legalities, I'd just get on with it. In some ways it was completely reckless.

In other ways, though, I was quite shy. I did once summon up the courage to ask one of Beech House's maids, a girl called Gwendoline, to meet me behind the school pavilion, but we just spent all our time talking about when we could see each other again. I wasn't helped by the fact that two of my friends were hiding behind nearby bushes and sniggering. I never did date Gwendoline again, though she always smiled at me in the school corridors.

My fears and unanswered questions apart, the last years of Rydal were enjoyable. I was a prefect and head of house and played for the school at cricket and rugby. Most of the time in my last year of sixth form was spent playing canasta, which was all the rage.

I had also developed a passion for the cinema. Every Saturday night in the winter term at Rydal films would be shown in the school hall. Abbott and Costello, Laurel and Hardy, Will Hay and Old Mother Riley were my favourites – all the old films of the '30s.

When I was in the sixth form, most afternoons my friends and I were able to go out to the matinées in Colwyn Bay. We were only supposed to go four times a term by special pass, but we were never caught. Of course it all mounted up and wasn't cheap. Often we would club together to buy a single ticket and one of us would go in, nip to the loo and open the fire door to the rest of us. Anyone seeing one boy go into the toilet and six come out would have wondered what was going on, but we were never caught at that either. I probably saw more films in those two years than I have in all the years since.

The film that excited me beyond measure was *The Jolson Story*, a musical about Al Jolson's life. There was one scene where as a young boy he suddenly stood up in a theatre and started to sing. He had a beautiful voice and I remember thinking, *My God, if I only could stand up and sing like that...* I recognized then the exhibitionism involved in acting – the showman side of it, the showing off, all the things that I can't be. It's a very immature thing really. But I walked out of the cinema absolutely enthralled with his performance. Jolson was a great showman – he was the first entertainer to have a causeway constructed in the theatres where he appeared so he could go out and get right amongst his audience. He would take any song and hit it beautifully, just punch it over to the audience, and all you could do was take it and enjoy it, and you wouldn't have it any other way. That was the impact of that man and I absolutely loved him. I bought not only every record of his I could lay my hands on but also the sheet music, which I would hammer out on the piano and play on the trumpet.

Later of course I found out that he was an absolute monster – a horrendous guy! He would take songs that people had written and give them virtually nothing for them. He would insist his name was put on them as joint writer... But to be like that, to have that confidence and that dash, you've got to have a sort of arrogance, I suppose.

I thought that all actors were full of confidence. That's why, in spite of the acting I'd done and the prize I'd received, I thought I'd be no good at it. Actors seemed to have lots of self-confidence and personality, and I was very shy. So, although I longed to be an actor, I thought it was an unrealistic ambition, just a dream. I didn't tell anyone about it.

By then my sister had left school and gone on to agricultural college. There she met a fellow student and they got married. My father helped set them up in a little 40-acre farm in Markfield, Leicestershire. They bred pigs and it was a pretty tough existence, but they managed to keep going.

I was taking chemistry, biology and physics in the sixth form and the idea was that I would follow in the footsteps of my father and grandfather and get a place at St Bartholomew's. Although my heart was not committed to medicine, my august predecessors were a persuasive presence.

I disliked chemistry and physics, but enjoyed biology. It was taught by Mrs Olive James, who was a war widow, I believe. She gave me extra tuition at her house in Llandudno and I liked her very much. She also liked me, but I didn't have the confidence to take anything further. However, I got a good grade in my biology exam, though not in physics and chemistry. I would have to retake those before I could go to Bart's.

Then fate intervened. During the summer holidays I received my call-up papers for National Service.

Part II

Army Dreaming

*'Welcome the challenges
that Earth has to offer.'*

CHAPTER 4

Training to Kill

'Every problem is a challenge not only to be met and accepted but also to be overcome. Thus the indwelling spirit grows and unfolds.'

National Service would last for two years. Registering for the army from school would mean joining one of the Welsh regiments, the most likely being the Royal Welch Fusiliers, as their HQ was in Wrexham. We were still at war with North Korea, which was showing no sign of ending, and the RWF were very much involved.

During my last year at school I saw boys leaving and going into the army and a lot of them coming back as officers in their smart uniforms. They looked pretty impressive. I thought, *I wonder if I'll ever get commissioned?* I remember sitting at my sixth-form desk during the summer term and thinking that in a matter of weeks I could be out fighting in Korea. It was a sobering thought, but strangely I was not afraid.

War still seemed very distant to me and I never really thought about what it involved. It may sound naïve, but I never thought about the army being a killing machine. It was just something you went to from school. You had to enlist and I did it. It was a process that was happening, something that was inevitable, so there was no point worrying about it.

'Worry is bad for you. It blocks the channel
by which help can come.'

In fact, from going through a period of enquiry, I went into a period where I put my questions on hold and just dealt with whatever life presented me with. Although the purpose of life is the unfolding of the spirit, we only become aware of this when we are ready. Before we gain this awareness, we grow by overcoming the experiences that life puts in front of us. That's the process I was about to go through.

My first day in the army is still clear in my mind. It was Thursday 3 January 1952. My parents put me on the train to Wrexham with just a small suitcase containing the basic requirements. I had no idea what to expect. I left my watch and fountain pen at home because I was afraid they might be stolen. I was to arrive at Hightown Barracks any time before but not a minute after 16.00 hours.

The train arrived at Wrexham at around 2 p.m. and as I walked up the platform I quickly became aware that I was part of an easily identifiable group. There were about five other white-faced 18-year-olds wearing raincoats and carrying small suitcases.

Standing by the exit to the station was a sergeant wearing a red sash. With him were two fusiliers and behind them on the road stood a three-ton truck. This was the reception party to ferry the doomed to the barracks. I did a smart left turn into the refreshment room and waited until they had gone. Determined to enjoy my last moments of freedom, I ordered a cheese and onion roll and a cup of tea. After this I sauntered around Wrexham, found the barracks and, at five minutes to four, took a deep breath and walked nervously past the guard and into the unknown.

'With open eyes, an open heart and courage flowing freely, turn to face your fear.'

Luckily, I was more prepared than I knew. In a way it was almost like starting school all over again. I'm quite sure being at public school helped me in the army. I was already used to being away from my family and fitting in wherever I went. This time, though, I was known as 22626311 Fusilier Roache rather than Fish. And we had to do everything at the double.

The six weeks of basic training were tough. The new boots were a particular nightmare until they had been broken in, and then they became my best friends – except when they had to be 'bulled up' for a parade.

What amazed me more than anything else about the army was the language. Previously, rude words had been whispered with a giggle and surreptitiously looked up in the reference library. Now the NCOs were shouting them at us all the time. That was a sort of convention, though, and didn't actually seem offensive. It was as if the NCOs were playing a part. But my fellow fusiliers swore all the time. At first this really took me aback. I was not only staggered by the number of rude words but also how they were used – not to be rude or to emphasize something, but simply as part of everyday speech. After the first few days, though, even this became part of my new life and passed unnoticed.

First of all we were taught how to fall in, stand to attention, stand at ease, march with a straight back and arms and turn to the left and right. It wasn't long before we were able to dress, march and salute like real soldiers, so we were allowed out of barracks in our spare time. The uniform was very smart and good for going out in the evening and I was already beginning to feel very different from the schoolboy of only a few weeks ago.

The advanced battle training in preparation for Korea was looming. This was to be done in Brecon, South Wales.

The accommodation at Brecon was a bit of shock, as it was a large wooden hut with a concrete floor. The only heating was a pot-bellied stove, and the ventilator at one end of the hut had been knocked out. Flurries of snow were coming in through the hole. The first night we slept in all our clothes, including our greatcoats.

At Brecon we were taught to fire the 303 rifle, the Bren gun and the two-inch mortar, and to throw hand grenades and do bayonet charges. The charges involved running towards a suspended sack of straw and thrusting the bayonet into it, then pausing, twisting, withdrawing the bayonet and running on. We were told to shout while we did it.

We were being trained to kill, but it all just seemed like a big game. Firing on the range at targets was like a grown-up fairground, throwing hand grenades was a bit dodgy but fun, and the bayonet charges made us laugh because of all the shouting. We never considered the real end result of these activities. We were like schoolboys at play.

'A fool laughs at he knows not what.'

But all too soon it would be real. The platoon with which I trained eventually went to Korea and four of my colleagues were killed.

That young men, not long out of school, should die in a distant land for some remote reason is an abomination. I believe there is no such thing as a just war. If the United Nations could become more powerful and more honourable, then it would be able to deal with rogue nations and settle disputes between countries, and war would become obsolete. Providing countries abided by the rules and did not act unilaterally, of course.

I did not go to war with my fellow fusiliers, as on arrival at Brecon a few of us were taken out and put into a potential leaders' platoon. We were considered to be possible officer material. The reason for this, among other things, was that we had passed the school certificate.

There was an amusing incident when we were all standing by our beds and a corporal was going round checking our educational qualifications to make sure we were eligible for the platoon. To him, the school certificate was the ultimate academic achievement.

Eventually, arriving at the last bed, he said to the fusilier standing there, 'Have you got your school certificate?'

The fusilier answered, 'Well actually, corporal, I've got a First Class honours degree in English and history from Cambridge University.'

The corporal shouted, 'Don't try to get out of it! *Have you got your school certificate?*'

We were all waiting to be called for WOSBY, the War Office Selection Board, which was a three-day examination to see if we were suitable material to be turned into officers and gentlemen. We were all called up at different times and when one of the group came back he would be subjected to an intense barrage of questions as we tried to extract from him every minute detail of the process.

In the meantime the commanding officer at Brecon was an ill-tempered major waiting for retirement who found the PL platoon the perfect object on which to work out his anger and frustration. So every day started out with latrine duties, followed by whatever demeaning task he could find or create.

It was unpleasant, but I'm a great believer that if you're in a position you have to be in, you should make the best of it. National Service was compulsory, so there we were. Of course some people did kick against it all the way through. But they got little benefit from it and were nothing but trouble for everyone else. I saw little point in making life even more difficult than it already was. So I just got on as best I could and did the best I could.

'If earthly life were easy and everyone were materially rich and had no problems, then spiritually you would be puny weaklings.'

After a few weeks at Brecon, not yet three

months into my army career, I was surprisingly promoted to lance corporal. All it meant, though, was that I was a glorified dormitory monitor who was responsible for getting everyone in the right place at the right time. There were usually about 12 of us in the platoon, mostly ex-public schoolboys, and people were leaving and arriving all the time, so you just had to keep track and make sure everyone knew the ropes.

On one of our nights off I met a very attractive girl in one of the local pubs and we met up several times before I was posted out of the area. I was still quite shy where women were concerned, but had also met a girl called Kath at a New Year's Eve dance in Ilkeston and was keeping in touch with her. Gradually I was gaining confidence.

I had to suffer several weeks of latrine duties in the PL platoon, so I was relieved when my call for WOSBY came, although this was tempered by a lot of anxiety.

WOSBY was a very unreal three days. It took place at Barton Stacey camp, near Andover. We had to wear a tabard with a large number on the front and the back so that we could be identified at all times. I was number 42 and felt like something out of *Alice in Wonderland*.

There were ten of us in the group and we were given a variety of tests and trials. On each occasion one of us would be called by number to take charge, except for one trial, when no one was put in charge, as this was designed to discover the natural leaders. This became a pushing, pulling, shouting match as each person tried to dominate the group. I remained silent during this struggle, as it all seemed very undignified, but felt that I had probably lost some points.

It was a very tense time. The tests were bad enough, but there was the added stress of knowing that we were under constant observation, even during rest periods and meals.

When it was my turn to take charge of a trial, we were all assembled by two trees 15 feet apart. The idea was that there was an imaginary fast-flowing river between these trees and all the men had to cross from one side to the other, with dry rifles, using just a length of rope.

I started off by asking, 'Who's a strong swimmer?'

Silence. It wasn't in anyone's interest to help me out. I turned to one of the group who had been in the Marines for two years. I felt fairly sure he would be able to swim. It turned out he could.

'Give your rifle to the man next to you,' I said, 'tie this rope around your waist and swim across. We'll have the other end of the rope so you won't be swept away.'

While the man was pretending to swim across the river, we tied the other end of the rope around one of the trees. Then I shouted across to him to tie his end around the other tree. I ordered all the men to put their rifles on their backs and cross the river hand over hand.

This seemed to go very well and in no time at all we were all on the other side of the river. I was feeling quite pleased with myself until the captain pointed out that the rope was still tied to the tree on the opposite side...

Group debates, map-reading, delivering a five-minute speech and a written examination all followed. Then on the morning of the third day came an individual interview by a board of eight officers. This was easily the most daunting of all the events. The style of questioning was quite relaxed, but knowing that so much depended on the result made us all nervous.

I can't remember many of the questions, but at one point one of the officers asked me whether I would be prepared to give an order for corporal punishment.

'If I felt it was necessary,' I said.

I didn't add that I couldn't imagine when it would ever be necessary.

After these interviews there was lunch and then we were told to line up outside, where we would be given our results. Instant execution.

We lined up in numerical order and the captain who had been in charge of us walked down the line handing each of us a slip of paper. On it was our name and number and three short sentences:

- 'Recommended for officer cadet training.'
- 'Not recommended for officer cadet training.'
- 'Recommended to try again in six months.'

Two of the sentences would be crossed out.

I was towards the end of the line and watched as each of my fellow hopefuls received their slips. The results weren't in an envelope or folded, so they could be seen before being handed to you.

The first man looked straight back at the

captain and then at the rest of us. A pass. The second smiled. A pass. The third looked down at the floor. A fail. The fourth stood defiantly erect and stared into the middle distance. A fail. So far a 50 per cent fail rate. My heart was thudding. The fifth man smiled broadly. A pass. The sixth man bent his head. A fail. He was crying. The seventh looked at his paper and gave a hollow laugh. Try again.

Now it was my turn. I held my breath. As the captain approached me, I saw my paper. It had the second and third lines crossed out. Joy and relief flooded through me. I had been recommended for officer training. I think that was when I first realized that I must be quite a good actor.

I was sent home on leave for a fortnight. It was summer, my father had bought me a motorbike and I got to know Kath very well indeed. Life seemed pretty good.

However, there now loomed the four-month officer cadet training, which would not only be rigorous but also have the sword of Damocles hanging over it in the form of being RTU'd. Being 'returned to unit' meant you had absolutely no chance of ever being commissioned.

My officer cadet school was no less than

the Duke of Westminster's stately home, Eaton Hall in Cheshire, which was only a short distance from the depot at Wrexham. Having sent my luggage ahead in an army truck, I rode there on my treasured Francis Barnett motorbike.

The journey only took 20 minutes. It was Sunday and it was pleasantly quiet. Arriving at Eaton Hall, I saw a huge red-brick Victorian building with some huts in front of it. I wasn't sure where to park my bike, but then I saw an area of tarmac beyond the huts, so I accelerated towards it.

Suddenly I found myself in a vast open space. I had ridden onto the parade square! This was the ultimate sacrilege. It was forbidden to even step on the square unless it was for an official duty. Worse, a sergeant was drilling a squad on it, and before I could stop myself I had ridden straight between them. Sergeants prided themselves on the strength of their voices and demonstrated this by standing as far away as possible from the squad they were drilling, so riding between them was easily done.

Utterly panic-stricken, I roared away with the sergeant's stream of abuse ringing in my ears.

You've done it this time, Roache, I thought.

You'll be RTU'd on your first day!

Finding somewhere to park my bike at last, I went into the main building. I was told where my room was and to take my battle-dress uniforms to the camp tailor to have the officer cadet's white collar tabs sewn on. I wondered whether it was worth it.

> *'There will always be problems while you are on Earth, because your world is where you learn your lessons.'*

As I was unpacking, an awesome figure marched into my room. It was the sergeant. I now realized he was from the Coldstream Guards. These were a very different breed of soldier from the one I was used to. They were immaculately dressed, ramrod straight and quite intimidating.

'Officer Cadet Roache?'

'Yes, sergeant.'

'You had the audacity to drive your infernal machine across the square while I was on it, didn't you, sir?'

'Yes, sergeant.'

'Be at the company office at 09.25 tomorrow morning for company orders.'

'Yes, sergeant.'

On his way out, he turned back. 'Bloody

good start to your training, isn't it, sir?'

I had never heard the word 'sir' used quite so effectively as an insult. I was absolutely certain that the very next day I would be returning to my unit.

At the company office the next morning the sergeant was waiting for me, along with the company sergeant major. The CSM marched me in, and there was a major, sitting at a table with a dog by his side. The CSM explained the charges. I stood there expecting the worst.

Then the sergeant himself was brought in.

'Right, sergeant,' said the major. 'Tell me what happened.'

'*Yes, sir!*' the sergeant shouted. He gave all his evidence at full blast, finishing with: 'Never in all my time in the army have I witnessed anything like this, sir! It showed disrespect for me, the army and all that I believe in, sir! I felt humiliated, sir! My authority was undermined, sir!'

The major seemed slightly pained by all the noise. He dismissed the sergeant and said simply, 'Well, Roache, what the devil were you doing?'

My hopes rose. I explained briefly and apologized.

The major leaned back in his chair. There was a definite twinkle in his eye. 'You're not going to make a habit of this, are you, Roache?'

'Definitely not, sir!'

'All right, you'd better stay in camp for a week. Now off you go, there's a good chap.'

Someone was looking after me.

Now I know that in fact we all have guides and helpers around us all the time. At Eaton Hall I was a long way from this realization, though. I just had to focus on what I was doing. The work was hard and if you fell behind you were jumped on severely, but everyone appreciated the need for this and gave their all. We were well aware that in future we could be making decisions upon which the lives of 40 men depended.

There was relentless pressure on us to keep up to the mark and with the ever-present threat of being RTU'd, the stress was palpable. There had been two suicides from the intakes just before ours, there was one while I was there and I heard of another after I had left. The cadet who committed suicide while I was at Eaton Hall had in fact been offered a commission but not in the regiment he wanted and he could not face the 'shame' he had brought on his family.

At the time I felt saddened by the suicides, but other than that I didn't think too much about them. All through the army it was almost as if I was dreaming my way through life. I lived through things but did not enquire into their meaning. I have since read that the early part of your life can be a recapitulation of something that happened before, and it may well be that I had a past life at some time in the army. Whatever the reason, I know it was all meant to be. It was often a pressurized life as an officer cadet, but it was part of the life that I had chosen before I incarnated.

People often ask why we choose to experience pressures and difficulties. I believe that you're never given more than you can bear. But sometimes spirits are very eager to learn and move forward and when they choose the circumstances and events of their lives, they will load themselves up a little too much and push themselves a little too far. Suicide is a case in point. All it means is that someone has given themselves a test and it has been too much for them. That's all. There's no punishment for that. It's ridiculous that the Church says that suicides can't be buried on sanctified ground. All that has happened is that they have given themselves too much and haven't been able to cope with it. So in their next life they'll be given more help and will be presented with those challenges in a way that they can manage. If you fail an exam, you're given extra tuition, and for a suicide it's the same. They'll be given extra help and extra love.

At Eaton Hall the day of the passing-out parade arrived. This was when we would receive Her Majesty's commission. Our parents attended the parade, as did various other members of the public and a selection of high-ranking officers. Beforehand we took our uniforms to the tailor to have our regimental pips sewn on. When we collected them afterwards we saw, with great pride, our new rank emblazoned on the epaulettes.

Now that I was commissioned, I felt I could give some thought to my future and I decided to take a short service commission for five years. I had realized that I didn't really want to be a doctor, but I did feel a certain obligation to uphold the family honour in some way. My family history had been army, church and medicine, like a lot of families. So by being commissioned in the army I was still part of the family tradition. I'm not quite sure why that was important, but it was.

Fortunately, my parents weren't upset about my decision not to take up medicine. They were kind people and really just wanted to make sure I was doing what I wanted. Life was changing rapidly for them too. The National Health Service was just coming in and the private practice that had been handed down for generations was now gone. My father sold Rutland House the same year that I was commissioned, 1952, to his then assistant and soon afterwards moved to a bungalow he had had built in Trowell, a village between Ilkeston and Nottingham. He paid half of the proceeds of the sale to Uncle John, who had recently retired from the army, in the hope that it would set him up. To the family's surprise he did join Alcoholics Anonymous and manage to get a job. He rented a rather squalid room in Nottingham and took up with a prostitute, though apparently she still charged him for her services.

Back at Rutland House, the former assistant had some problems with alcohol and became reclusive. The garden and the house were left unattended and both deteriorated. Years later, after he had died and the house become uninhabitable, I would go there.

The house was boarded up and the gates locked, but I would climb over the wall and walk about the old garden. Apart from being overgrown, it was untouched from the time when it was my childhood playground. I found the rusted remains of the swing and the remnants of the sandpit and once, pulling back the tangled branches of an overgrown bush, I found an old tennis ball. I recognized it as one that I used to hit against the house, and childhood memories came flooding back. It was like Miss Havisham's house in *Great Expectations*.

By that time Michael House School had moved and had sold its premises to Weleda, the manufacturers of homoeopathic remedies. They, in turn, eventually bought up the now desolate Rutland House and, having demolished it, used the area to extend their premises. Given that my grandfather had given the land in the first place and had an interest in homoeopathy, it had come full circle.

Sadly, there is now no trace of Rutland House or the garden of my childhood memories.

Life is always changing and it is up to us to make the best of the situations in which we find ourselves. I feel that wherever you are you should look for the good, do your best and make what contribution you can to society. I always felt that I wanted to help and give in some way. I think that came from the fact that my family were doctors, so I had a tradition of service around me as I was growing up. If it hadn't been for National Service, I'd never have considered the army as a career. But there I was, and as well as being an opportunity for service, it was a chance to see the world and learn a bit more about life.

After the passing-out parade, we rushed to the notice board to find out the regiment and location of our posting. As far as I knew, all the Royal Welch Fusilier battalions were in Korea and I was expecting to be sent there.

There was a scramble around the notice board and it was some time before I was near enough to see the list. Eventually I read: 'Second Lieutenant W.P. Roache. Posting. 2nd Battalion, Royal Welch Fusiliers. Caribbean.'

Caribbean? I didn't really know what that meant. Was there a war zone in the area? After a few enquiries I found to my delight that the battalion was stationed in Kingston, Jamaica.

CHAPTER 5

Cricket and Fireworks

'God does not inflict suffering but uses the suffering man creates for himself to bring good into the individual's life.'

I spent a final Christmas at Rutland House and reported to Stansted Airport on 7 January 1953. I was trying not to let it show, but I was feeling very nervous, as this was the first time I had ever flown and I didn't really know what to expect. I was directed to a Nissen hut where I met my fellow travellers, mainly NCOs and other ranks. Eventually an RAF sergeant led us across the tarmac to the only plane in sight – an ancient camouflaged Hudson bomber. I knew what it was because I'd made a model of one at school. Hudsons were powered by two propeller-driven engines. My heart sank at the thought that this was how we were going to cross the Atlantic.

Inside the plane there were seats made of

canvas stretched over a tubular steel frame. Our luggage was strapped down behind us. That was it. It was pretty basic.

'The stones on the roadway from which you shrink, they are the spirit's choice.'

We settled down and the ground crew began fuelling the plane. While this was taking place, a piece of equipment crashed into one of the propellers. This caused some consternation and after some thought one of the crew produced a hammer and hit the end of the propeller with it. The pilot climbed into the plane and started that engine. Then he stopped it, climbed back out and everyone gathered round the propeller once more. One of the mechanics reached out to touch it and pulled his hand back quickly. It was obviously very hot. They hit it with the hammer again.

None of this improved my state of mind and I was feeling very insecure when we took off for Reykjavik, Iceland, on the first leg of our journey. I sat quietly and hoped for the best. In fact the engines were so noisy that conversation was impossible, although the pilot did walk back and shout at us a couple of times.

I was very relieved when we arrived safely at Reykjavik and were taken to the American airbase. As it turned out, we were there for five days because there was a mechanical fault with the Hudson and spare parts had to be flown out for it.

Eventually we took off again, this time for Halifax, Nova Scotia. It was cold, dark and uncomfortable in the plane and after about two hours it started shuddering more than usual. No one knew what this meant. I was terrified.

After a while the pilot came back and yelled that we were just off the foot of Greenland, but the headwinds were so strong that we were hardly moving and would have to turn back.

We spent another two days in Reykjavik waiting for better weather conditions. Then we set off again.

Once we had actually made it to Halifax, we were told that the plane had another mechanical fault. It was another six days before we were able to take off for Kingston. The flight that should have taken a few hours had actually taken 13 stressful days. After that, it was surprising that I didn't add flying to my collection of fears.

The first thing that hit me on arrival in Jamaica was the heat. It was sweltering. The second thing was the smell, a mixture of spices and fish. It was strong, but not unpleasant.

We were met by two second lieutenants, a duty sergeant and four men. While the sergeant was sorting everyone out, one of the second lieutenants came over and introduced himself as Selwyn Hughes. He was pleased to see me because up to that point he had been the junior subaltern and now that would be me.

There is always a reason why people cross your path. It is either to teach you something or for you to teach them something, and so it was to prove with Selwyn. I warmed to him straightaway.

I was taken to the officers' mess sleeping quarters at Up Park Camp. Nearly all the buildings were made of wood and perched on raised posts. Each room had a verandah, a large fan in the ceiling and a mosquito net over the bed. It all seemed very different from what I'd been used to but exactly how I would have expected things to be in a hot country.

Selwyn took me to the mess and we had banana sandwiches and fresh orange juice with sugar served in silver goblets. This was the usual teatime fare. I was also introduced to rum with fresh lime and sugar. This became a favourite drink, and it was a highly deceptive one, as you could barely taste the rum but would soon find yourself sliding into a pleasant haze. Getting smashed on a nightly basis was a pleasure back then but the following days' hangovers would be horrendous. It took me years to find out you didn't have to have one.

Jamaica was independent by then and was part of the Commonwealth. We were basically stationed there for anything that might occur in the Caribbean. We were responsible for the security of the area.

On the first morning I reported to Battalion HQ at 10.00 hours to meet my commanding officer, Lieutenant Colonel Johnson. He was the highest-ranking officer I had so far met, apart from the WOSBY board, and I was expecting to take immediate command of 40 men, one sergeant and three corporals.

Nothing in all the months of officer cadet training prepared me for this meeting.

I stamped to attention and saluted.

'Hello, Mr Roache,' said Colonel Johnson pleasantly. He was a thickset man with close-cropped fair hair. He got up and walked round his desk to greet me and I was stunned to realize he was wearing a very colourful floral shirt, khaki shorts and sandals.

'Come and sit down, and welcome to the battalion. Do you play bridge?'

'Yes, colonel.'

'Good show. Now I expect all my junior officers to play polo, so report to the stables sometime this week and they will sort you out. I am sending you to B Company under Major Tolhurst, but we are very under-strength at the moment, so you won't be getting a platoon. But I do have a sergeant for you, and there is something that I want you to do. We are going to have a military tattoo to celebrate the coronation of the Queen. In a few days £4,000 worth of fireworks will arrive by ship. They are made up of two £2,000 displays each with a 16-foot portrait of Her Majesty, but as the tattoo is to last for four days, they are to be broken down into four displays. Obviously, there are only two portraits, so I suggest that these are used on the first and the last day. As well as your sergeant you can have the full use of the battalion carpenter to make whatever devices or supports you may need. Well, I've got a polo game to prepare for, so you get off and show your face to B

Company, and good luck.'

With that he walked out, leaving me to contemplate the organization of a firework display. It was certainly not what I had expected.

My sergeant, Sergeant Duffissey, was an old soldier who, sadly, was too fond of his beer. He had had an interesting war, though, and would tell some good stories which, even allowing for exaggeration, were fascinating.

One of them particularly intrigued me. As Sergeant Duffissey told it, he and two other men had been crossing an open field in France when a sniper fired at them from the ruins of an old farmhouse. They instantly dropped down, but there was little cover so they were left partly exposed as they returned the fire.

A few shots were exchanged and the men were wondering whether they should make a dash for better cover when a rabbit suddenly appeared on the left side of the field, between them and the sniper.

As the rabbit started to make its way across the field, a shot rang out from the sniper, just missing the rabbit. After a pause the sergeant and his colleagues all fired at the rabbit, also missing. The sniper fired again and so did they, and they all kept firing and missing until the rabbit reached safety on the other side of the field.

There was a long pause. Then the sniper slowly stood up, not holding his rifle. Cautiously, Sergeant Duffissey and the other men also got to their feet. For a while they looked straight at the sniper and he looked back. Then he waved, they waved back and they all started laughing. Then, with a final wave, they all went on their way.

I loved this story. It reminded me of the football match on Christmas Day in the First World War when the British and German troops climbed out of their opposing trenches and got together to swap cigarettes and pieces of cake before forming two teams to have a game of soccer. I'm not sure what happened to the German soldiers afterwards but the British troops had to be replaced – they had simply lost the will to kill. Now that's what I call a touching story.

I enjoyed working with the fireworks. The CO had personally selected them and continued to take a huge interest in the whole project. Every day he asked me for a progress report. When the fireworks arrived he took me down to a warehouse in the docks where they were being loaded onto lorries by a group of fusiliers. He had one of the crates opened, reached inside and reverently lifted out a five-foot rocket with an 18-inch head. Holding it up in triumph, he beamed, *'Magnificent.'*

In view of the obviously high expectations, I planned the display with the utmost care. The battalion carpenter built racks to hold the large rockets and made other frames and stands for the rest of the weird and wonderful assortment and a 30-foot bamboo tower to hold the burning portraits of Her Majesty. I had arranged for all the rockets on the racks to be set off in small groups, and the plan was that Sergeant Duffissey would light them and I would rush around lighting the bigger fireworks in between each group.

The big day arrived and everything was ready. The frames, stands and tower were all in place and the audience was waiting expectantly. The battalion fire engine was standing by as a precaution – fortuitously, as it happens. It was all systems go, except that my sergeant had disappeared. I suspected he was in the mess, drinking his favourite Red Stripe beer, and sent an urgent message there. I was starting to panic, as he was the only person who knew the routines.

With less than five minutes to go, I saw him stumbling towards me.

'Where the hell have you been?'

'Shorry, shurr,' he mumbled.

'Can you remember what to do?'

'Yeshsir...'

There was less than a minute to go.

'Right. Well, go and stand by the rockets and wait for my signal.'

When I saw that he was standing in the right place and had lit his fuse, I raised my arm and dropped it. This was the pre-arranged signal for him to light the first batch of rockets on the rack.

He did successfully light the first rocket, but then as he moved to the second one he staggered, knocking the already lit rocket down onto the rack. Its long tail of fire and sparks streamed down the whole length of the rack, setting off all the rockets in one go.

I was horrified. The only thing I could think of was trying to preserve the sequence. I ran around setting off all the big spec-tacular fireworks as quickly as I could. What was to have been a ten-minute display was over in two minutes. And the rocket rack was on fire.

I was standing forlornly in my scorched

shirt watching the fire engine extinguish the remaining flames on the rocket rack when to my horror I saw Colonel Johnson striding towards me. As if I had not had enough rockets for one day, here was another one.

He marched straight up to me. 'Well done, Mr Roache. Much better than I expected. Keep it up.' I was stunned.

There was only one thing to do – for the remaining three nights the firework display was only two minutes long. But spectacular.

Eventually I acquired about half a platoon and fairly normal soldiering resumed. I say 'fairly normal' because my company commander, Major Tolhurst, commonly known as Guy, also ran the battalion cricket team and had heard that I had played cricket for my school. He believed that cricket was more important than soldiering, and as most Jamaicans believed that cricket was more important than anything, he was in the right country.

So it was that I found myself playing cricket three or four days a week, like it or not. Every plantation in Jamaica had a cricket field. They were not quite up to Lord's standard – they could be sloping and bumpy, and one even had a tree in the middle – but the matches were always played with great enthusiasm.

To be honest, sometimes it was not apparent when the match had ended and the party had begun. Drinks would be brought onto the pitch at regular intervals, usually laced with rum, and the inevitable steel band would start playing in the early evening whatever the state of the game. The party would then continue late into the night.

If we weren't on the cricket field, we'd spend our evenings at the officers' club, where rum was tuppence a tot, so to wake up in the morning without a hangover was a very rare event. I really used to think that if we ever had to go to war, I might be safer on the other side.

As a junior officer I found my army pay would barely cover the drinks bill in the mess and I began to be worried about having to play polo, as it was fairly costly, with all the equipment and the upkeep of the horses. In the end I was quite relieved to discover that I would not be able to play after all, because of being left-handed. Apparently it would cause difficulties with the horse and lead to an infringement of the offside rule. I was amused to find my earlier 'problem' now working to my advantage.

By now Selwyn and I had become great friends and were spending a lot of time in each other's company. He also had half a platoon to command and in his spare time was writing poetry. He was very bright and hoping to go to university. In comparison I was just drifting along from day to day.

My time in Jamaica was for the most part enjoyable, in spite of the hangovers. The most alarming moment was when I woke up once in the middle of the night and saw something dark, about the size of a tennis ball, slowly crawling up the mosquito net just above my face. Tarantulas were quite common and I started to panic. Very slowly, I reached out of the net and switched on the light. It was the mess kitten.

The two major incidents the battalion was involved with at the time were providing the security for the Big Three conference in Bermuda and going to Georgetown, British Guyana, to put down a rebellion.

The 'Big Three' in Bermuda were Churchill, Eisenhower and the French premier Joseph Laniel, and the talks were held at the Mid Ocean Golf Club. Our duties weren't that arduous and we found the Bermudan people very friendly. Selwyn and I were invited out to dinner most evenings. Our hosts were invariably fascinated by everything British and would jump up to drink a toast at the mere mention of anything to do with royalty or the homeland. We once drank a toast to hunt balls.

We also had the opportunity to get to know the 18-year-old twin daughters of a rich diamond dealer quite well, only Selwyn took it all too far and told them he was the Right Honourable Selwyn and I was Lord Roache of Nottingham. We had to avoid them after that in case we were found out.

Almost as soon as we got back to Jamaica we heard that the governor of British Guyana had called us in because he thought the policies of the prime minister, Cheddi Jagan, were undermining his authority and might provoke an uprising. In preparation we did two battalion exercises. These were a complete shambles, or rather the first one was. The second one was called off because it was raining.

The whole battalion, getting on for 1,000 men, went to British Guyana to support the governor, but all we did was march through the centre of Georgetown and hope that we looked impressive enough to prevent a possible rebellion. It seemed to be successful. The only shot fired was by a major who accidentally shot his lieutenant in the leg as he was unloading his revolver. Fortunately it was just a flesh wound.

We were only in British Guyana for a couple of months. We played some cricket there and I went on a crocodile shoot down the Esequibo river, along with a sergeant and two fusiliers. Two Guyanese guides paddled us along in a small wooden canoe. For the most part the jungle came right down to the water's edge and at one point I saw an anaconda sliding down into the river. It seemed to go on forever and it was a little disconcerting to think of it somewhere under our flimsy wooden boat, knowing that it could swallow a man whole.

After around two hours we passed a mud bank on which a couple of alligators were basking. As we approached, one scuttled off into the water. I raised my rifle and fired at the other one. It rolled over and lay still. We pulled the boat up onto the bank and went over to have a look at it. It was about six feet long; not that big for an alligator, but I had got one. We laid it flat at the bottom of the canoe and decided we might as well have lunch now that we had stopped.

We wandered off to a nearby clearing and ate our packed lunches. When we came back to the canoe, ready to set off again, something was thrashing around in the bottom of it. The alligator was alive.

Fortunately the canoe was narrow and the alligator was confined under the seats, but although that meant it couldn't get out, it also meant we couldn't get in. We couldn't shoot it either, as a bullet-hole in the boat would have left us stranded.

After some thought we decided to make a noose to clamp the alligator's jaws shut so that we could hold its head over the side and shoot it. This took some doing, but eventually we managed it. I never liked killing but back then I did not have a true understanding of the sanctity of life.

After a year, the tour of duty in the West Indies was over and the battalion returned to the UK to take up temporary residence in an old army camp in Chiseldon. I came home a few weeks earlier to attend a three-inch mortar course and then to be part of the advance party to Chiseldon.

I had travelled home on a banana boat on which there were four cabin passengers and a number of Jamaicans travelling below deck in much more crowded conditions. It took 14 days and there was only one film, *Paleface* with Bob Hope. By the time we landed, I could have done a word-perfect recital of it.

On board the boat there was a wonderful moment that I shall never forget. On the evening of Christmas Day we all went below deck and joined the other passengers to sing carols. Imagine 'Away In A Manger' and 'Silent Night' being sung in a Caribbean rhythm along with the colourful appearance of those other passengers and you will understand why I found myself sobbing with joy. It was a beautiful moment. It brought back happy memories of childhood Christmases: we always had a huge tree and the presents would be piled up around it – I remember getting a little fort with soldiers one year, and a bike another. On Christmas Day we would always go up to the cottage hospital at Ilkeston where we would each receive a present from Father Christmas – it was years before I realized he was my father!

While I was on leave, Kath's mother asked me to go with her to a Spiritualist meeting at which she was a regular attender. I wasn't very enthusiastic, but I went out of politeness – after all, if your girlfriend's mother asks, you go, don't you? I sat at the back trying to be unobtrusive, but the medium, a gentle man in a navy suit, singled me out and said that he had someone for me who was wearing a long white coat and had something round his neck. This was a perfect description of a doctor with a stethoscope and I knew that if there was anyone who wanted to contact me it would be my grandfather.

'He's saying that you're at the bottom rung of a ladder,' the medium went on, 'and that if you hang on to it you'll get to the top. There are two maiden aunts looking after you. Three problems will affect your life. Two will be solved for you. The other you must solve yourself.'

Although a little embarrassed at being picked out, I was impressed. Two maiden aunts, Mickey and Mabel – my father's sisters had died when I was quite young and I later discovered that they had been Spiritualists. I did not, I hasten to add, ever discuss this with my father: he had a total lack of interest in such matters.

I eventually realized that the three problems were my fear of death, fear of infinity and a complete inability to accept most of the standard religious teachings. Years later, as I began to find some answers, the first two problems fell away. I am still working on the third, but more of that later.

I now realize that this meeting was an opportunity for me to start enquiring more deeply into things. It was something of a wake-up call. But at the time I totally ignored it.

Spiritualism does have a tremendous amount to offer, though it suffers from a poor image. Spiritualist churches are often perceived as places where people go just to get messages from the dead and are therefore seen as rather morbid. But there is so much more to it than that. These messages are proof of life in other realms, and receiving them should be the gateway to finding out more about these realms and about ourselves. This is precisely what I did not do, of course.

The beings from whom these messages come are not actually dead. In fact, the opposite is true – in many ways they are far more alive than we who are living in heavy material bodies on the Earth plane. Over the years some of them have passed on a great deal of information about life in the spiritual realms. These are much brighter and freer than our own. Death can be likened to walking out of a smoke-filled room into the fresh air. So Spiritualists can give an understanding of life after death and offer help to the grieving based on knowledge, not on superstition. They also teach many great truths and perform spiritual healing.

It is a shame that orthodox Christianity has branded Spiritualism as harmful and unhealthy. It is totally wrong to condemn it. In fact there was once a greater spirit of enquiry in the Church than there is today. In the '30s the Anglican Church set up a small commission of bishops to investigate whether or not Spiritualism should be accepted and encouraged. The majority of the commission found in favour of it, but no action was taken and their findings were suppressed. The Church is much the poorer for this action.

I myself was probably the poorer for not taking up the opportunity that was offered to me. I made up for lost time later on. But then I just pushed it all to the back of my mind. Life was moving on.

CHAPTER 6

Arabia

'Nothing happens without some purpose behind it. Experience should be made our own.'
Lao Tzu

I still had my fears of death and infinity. Sometimes I would get into such a state of fear that I would be close to passing out and would have to dash off to be somewhere on my own. I would think about how vulnerable we are, how terrifying infinity is. Those were the nights when I pictured that spaceship passing endlessly through galaxy after galaxy. The fear during these panic attacks was dreadful and there was no one I could talk to about it. I really thought that there was something seriously wrong with me. Absolutely no one, not even my parents, had any idea of what I was going through. Nowadays everyone knows about panic attacks and breathing into a brown paper bag to stop them, but at the time I thought that

I was alone in my condition. I thought it was something to be ashamed of, to keep secret, and that I would never be able to have a close relationship with anyone in case they found out. Looking back I can now see those two fears as great gifts: they led me to search for the answers I now have – and present in this book – that we are very limited here in this material and finite world whereas Spirit is infinite and open. I have grown to love infinity because if we didn't have it, God wouldn't be infinite, love wouldn't be infinite, life wouldn't be infinite, we wouldn't be infinite and everything would just end.

Fortunately the panic attacks were not frequent and I was always able to fulfil my duties. In fact they never happened if I was occupied. I soldiered on.

I reported to the Small Arms School for the three-inch mortar course and that turned out to be a life-changing experience.

Each mortar team was made up of three men. The mortar round itself was propelled by an explosive charge which ignited when the bomb reached the bottom of the barrel. On one occasion ours didn't go off. The procedure when this happened was to raise the barrel slightly and shake it, because usually the bomb had just got stuck. However, one of our team got carried away and pulled the mortar upright and shook it violently. The bomb went straight up into the air. And we were using live explosives.

I was standing quite near the mouth of the mortar at the time and the detonation blasted both of my eardrums, deafening me. Meantime the bomb was up in the air, we had no idea where it was going to come down and we only had about half a minute before it did. The sergeant in charge told us to get down. There was no point in running.

We all hit the deck and waited for what seemed like forever. Fortunately the bomb landed well away from us.

After that I was almost totally deaf for about three weeks and have had a permanent hearing problem ever since.

A much more pleasant experience was when the Queen visited us at Chiseldon to present the new colours to the regiment. I had the honour of carrying the old colours on the parade and afterwards we had lunch with Her Majesty. We had all met her only a few weeks before, when she had called at Kingston on her Commonwealth tour, and she commented that she could remember some of us, which especially pleased me because I remember on that first meeting having found her sexually very attractive. She would certainly have remembered the regimental goat, as I recall her laughing delightedly while offering it cigarettes to eat. This was the goat's party piece.

After a few weeks it was announced that the battalion would be moving to Dortmund in Germany. This didn't appeal to me at all. It would mean serious soldiering – combined exercises with the other NATO forces – and we would have to know what we were doing – something that we hadn't been used to for over a year.

To make matters worse, by the time we arrived in Germany it was winter, with grey skies most days. For a sun-lover like me it was not the best of places. So when I heard of a War Office request for volunteers to join the Trucial Oman Scouts, I could hardly wait.

I knew nothing about the Scouts other than they were a small Arab force with British officers whose role was to keep the peace between seven sheikhdoms in the Persian Gulf. Glubb Pasha ran a similar force in Jordan called the Arab Legion. I had visions of Beau Geste and Lawrence of Arabia and the romance of the hot desert sands. My heart started pounding – it was something that I had to do. Without making any proper enquiries, I went to the adjutant's office and volunteered.

'With the sword of truth and the shield of love, victory is assured.'

I had no real idea what to expect, nor what was expected of me. I was bewitched by the glamour and acted entirely on impulse. But was it impulse or intuition? In hindsight I would say more intuition. I had always felt an affinity with Egypt and the desert. Even now when I think of Egypt I feel a warm glow, but when I think of Roman times I get a grey feeling. I must have had a good life in Egypt, but not such a good one in Rome.

Within three weeks I was on embarkation leave and then two months after that I was travelling to Portsmouth to board a ship bound for Cairo.

Aboard the SS *Dilwara* was a battalion of the Leicestershire regiment heading for a tour of duty in Cairo. I was the only officer not of their regiment and found myself the object of much curiosity. 'I suppose you can't talk about what you're doing. Cloak and dagger stuff, eh?' one of their officers said to me. I didn't disillusion him, as I wasn't too sure of the nature of my work myself. Also the air of mystery that surrounded me meant I was left to my own devices and I enjoyed the freedom.

There were just two incidents on what was otherwise a pleasant and uneventful journey. Three of the officers' wives were not accompanied by their husbands, for some reason which I now forget, and we took to having drinks and dining together. There was nothing untoward in this and it was generally accepted to be no more than it seemed, but I was summoned to the CO's office one morning to be told that I was causing 'alarm and despondency' and would I 'not socialize with the wives'. Although it was innocent, it was apparently upsetting someone, and so these pleasant meetings came to an end. It was just as well that I didn't realize that this was to be my last contact with women for two years, or I might have been tempted further.

The other incident was the court martial of one of the privates in the Leicestershire regiment for having thrown all his kit out of a porthole. There were always three officers on a court martial and I was ordered to be one of them.

I was a lieutenant at the time and the other officers involved were a major and a captain. The procedure was that after all the evidence had been heard, which in this case was very little, the junior officer would give his verdict and punishment first. The army treated misuse of kit very seriously and I thought my two colleagues would be pretty severe on the private, although I didn't think that it was the worst crime in the world. His evidence had been that he thought the porthole was a cupboard, but clearly he had had a few beers too many.

I thought that I had better give a more severe punishment than I would like so as to be in line with the others. 'Three weeks' jankers,' I said, basically giving him three weeks of detention. It was with a mixture of embarrassment and relief that I listened to the others saying that that was far too severe and three days would be enough. So the private was not unduly punished.

We landed at Port Said and I was picked up by a small army vehicle and taken to a place called Faid in the canal zone.

Unfortunately we were not allowed out of the camp, so I missed an opportunity to see the pyramids and the Sphinx, but I did see the Nile. They say that if you see the Nile you will always return. This hasn't happened yet.

I had particularly wanted to see the mysterious Great Pyramid of Cheops, the only one of the Seven Wonders of the World that still exists. I have since read some esoteric writings on the pyramid and they all say that it was not built as a tomb, but as a storehouse of information and energy. The King's Chamber was an initiation chamber, where those who were ready could reach full enlightenment and be able to operate out of the body and on the astral plane. It was built by adepts with a mastery of mathematics and levitation. These masters were from Atlantis and were storing information in an indestructible form, as Atlantis was being destroyed by earthquakes, volcanic eruptions and floods.

Atlantis was a highly civilized society that was technically and spiritually advanced. Its centre was situated in the Atlantic and many storehouses were built in the outer regions and are still to be seen today, the pyramids of Mexico and Stonehenge being two of them. Atlantean technology was in its own way just as advanced and sophisticated as our own, but greed and pollution caused its destruction.

The first, and worst, pollution is the pollution of thought, followed by that of gas and chemicals and, of course, that all-inclusive polluter, war. Most people don't think of thought as a polluter, but the power of thought cannot be overestimated. Everything that exists started as a thought. And every thought that we have travels into the ether, followed by energy, takes shape and eventually returns to us, loaded with more of its kind. So is it any wonder that for the most part we are surrounded by a chaotic mist? And you can see how we get back what we send out.

The Earth's atmosphere is now chronically polluted by negative thoughts and a lot of hard work is needed through prayer and loving thought to dissipate this pollution. There are groups of people who do this, but we should all send loving thoughts to the Earth whenever we can. It is a wonderful living being. The arrangement is that it is there for our use and enjoyment, and in return we are to give it respect, care and love. This agreement has not been kept and after ages of abuse the Earth is now in a serious state of pollution. It will only take so much and then it will cleanse itself.

This is what brought about the fall of Atlantis. It was a very sophisticated civilization and technology had stormed ahead, but the people hadn't developed spiritually. They finally reached a point where greed and wrong thinking were so strong that the Earth had to cleanse itself of the pollution. So there were volcanic eruptions, earthquakes and floods, and Atlantis went down. A lot of its people died then, but not all. Some escaped and kept the knowledge that they had gained and passed it down. We are now in a similar state to that in Atlantis when it went down.

I didn't know all this when I was in Egypt, but I was still sorry not to see the pyramids.

After three weeks in Faid I was flown to Bahrain. From there I was put on an old clapped-out Anson for the flight to Sharjah, which I now knew to be my final destination.

They called the twin-engined Anson the cow of the air, as it was a wonderful worker whose parts could be replenished endlessly. The wings were a metal framework with cloth stretched over it, and on a subsequent journey back to Bahrain with the brigadier, who was Irish, a piece of the cloth ripped off and hung there, flapping in the slipstream. The brigadier shouted, 'My God, the cloth's coming off!' Amazingly, my overriding feeling was not panic or fear but fascination at the depth of his Irish accent.

On my first flight over the desert we were soon crossing endless but rather beautiful sand dunes. For a long while there was no sign of habitation. Then I saw a tiny grouping of huts made out of woven palm leaves and a piece of flattened sand marked out with old oil drums. That was the airstrip. I later found out the palm-leaf huts were known as *barusti* huts. As we came in to land we saw that they were laid out in a square around an area of well-flattened sand. This was apparently the drill square.

I clambered out of the Anson and was starting to walk towards the huts when I saw a slim fair-haired man walking towards me.

'Welcome, Captain Roache. I'm Colonel Johnson. Come into my office.'

He turned and led the way to one of the bigger *barusti* huts while I pondered two things: first, he had called me 'captain' but I was only a lieutenant, and second the fact that my commanding officer was again called Johnson.

This Colonel Johnson was very different from the first, however. There was an air of dedication and vocation about him. He could have been a priest. Sitting opposite this slim man with strong blue eyes in his bare office was very different from my Jamaican experience.

'We don't have any officers here under the rank of captain,' he told me. 'So your promotion has been authorized with effect from today.'

'Thank you, sir.'

'You will be taking over B squadron.'

Again, I thought. That was where the similarities ended, though.

'The squadron is made up of 140 Arabs, none of whom speak any English. You have a week to get to know the language. By the way, the previous commander was shot by his own men. Any questions?'

Yes, I thought, *what am I doing here?*

And yet strangely I knew that I was in the right place and that everything would work out as it should.

Not everyone was as enthusiastic about it, unfortunately. Kath wrote to me breaking off our relationship, saying in effect that anyone who wanted to go to a place like that must be a bit mad. She did have a point – I was going to be in the desert for two years, almost completely cut off from the rest of the world, with no leave at all. She could tell she wasn't my priority. And she wasn't. I was fond of her, but had no thoughts of settling down, and I really felt I had to go to the desert. It was a very strong impulse and was part, I think, of my past-life recapitulation. So she was absolutely right in what she did.

In the next week I learned as much basic Arabic as I could – words like 'food' and 'water', phrases like 'Where is...?' and of course the main greeting, *Salaam aleikum* (Peace be on you). Before I could draw breath I was in a Land Rover driving over the dunes to Mirfa to take command of my squadron.

The reason they were known as squadrons was because the command structure was based on tank regiments, which I presumed was due to the great tank battles that had taken place in the Western Desert in the Second World War. My squadron was mainly made up of Bedouin who had been sent to us by their sheikhs and told to obey us. There was also one Arab junior officer who could speak a little English (though he left after about a month), one sergeant major, four sergeants and six corporals. But none of them had been in the army for more than a year and they were all home-trained.

I am not a disciplinarian and favoured a laid-back approach. Fortunately for me, this was the right way and I was soon accepted by the men. The commander who had been shot had apparently made a lot of enemies by trying to impose strict military rules.

One thing I did notice was that if I gave an order to a sergeant, sometimes he would consult a private before carrying it out. Eventually I learned the reason for this. The Arabs' tribal hierarchy was very important to them and in that hierarchy a sergeant could sometimes be lower in rank than a private soldier. That was something you had to keep in mind.

Not long after I had taken command of my squadron we were told that a hunting party from Qatar, which was not part of the seven sheikhdoms, had trespassed into Oman. I had to track them down and to ask them to leave.

Taking about five Land Rovers full of men with me, I set off to look for the hunters' camp. Eventually we located it. I thought it best not to alarm them by arriving with all the soldiers, so I left most of them behind a sand dune and drove up to the camp with just the sergeant major and three men. The hunters greeted us respectfully and acknowledged that they had entered the territory of another sheikhdom, but when I formally requested that they leave, they stood their ground. They weren't being aggressive in any way, although they were heavily armed with rifles and daggers, but I was painfully aware that this was a delicate political situation and I didn't want to have an international incident on my hands.

Fortunately, at that moment the other Land Rovers suddenly pulled up. The sergeant I had left in charge had decided on his own initiative to come and back us up. I was very grateful that he did. At once the hunting party got into their vehicles and drove away.

Looking back, I think this situation was a lot riskier than I realized at the time. However, it passed off peacefully with both sides retaining their dignity, which was always of great importance to the Arabs.

The only other troublesome military incident occurred when two opposing groups laid claim to the Buraimi oasis, the only source of water for hundreds of miles. On that occasion we were actually involved in a battle, though it was rather a small one. Unfortunately both sides were dressed in civilian clothes, so it wasn't easy to tell them apart, and things got quite chaotic. We were supposed to be reclaiming the oasis and calming down the situation. We sent a few mortar shells up over the heads of the combatants and that did it – they surrendered. It was hardly the British army's finest hour, but the Prime Minister, Anthony Eden, did write to congratulate us.

Most of the time life was a lot quieter and in the evenings I enjoyed sitting around chatting to the men. Well, there was not much else to do. I didn't have a very good command of the language, but I could get by.

On one of these occasions I was trying to find out the Arabic for 'crab', as there were plenty of them scuttling around on the edge of the Gulf, I asked in my halting Arabic, 'What are those things with eight legs that scuttle about on the sand?'

To my surprise and dismay one of the men replied, *'Yehudi.'* Jew.

'Have you ever met a Jew?' I asked.

'No,' came the reply.

How was there ever going to be peace between the Arabs and the Jews when these

Bedouin who had never travelled out of their country were taught that Jews were monsters?

We were on the edge of the Rub al Khali, the Empty Quarter of the Arabian peninsula, and I also enjoyed going out into remote areas on my own. I would sit down on the sand and be filled with a wonderful feeling of peace. There was always total silence out there and I would relax completely. My mind would clear and it would seem that I could solve all my problems – overcome my fears of death and infinity, understand the purpose of life, even work out what to do with my career. I could sit there for hours and still not want to move.

I realize now that this was a type of untutored meditation. Had I known how to meditate I would have been able to use those surroundings much more effectively. But it was not until I was living in London many years later that I learned the art of meditation.

'You can struggle, have difficulties and battle, but you can still have tranquillity and peace.'

Meanwhile we carried on doing our patrolling and peace-keeping. It was a very basic life – sleeping in a tent or a *barusti* hut, eating the same food as the Arabs and only seeing another British officer once a month when he came with food supplies and pay. There was no entertainment, no alcohol, and the food was very frugal. Mainly it was rice flavoured with basil, and ghee, a kind of clarified butter. There was meat occasionally when a goat was killed. This was something that I always avoided seeing.

The Arabs would eat any animals that they caught. Once one of them brought me a jerboa in a trap, expecting me to have it cooked. That I was not about to do. A jerboa is a rat-like animal but they are very sweet, they eat with their hands like squirrels. So I made a little cage and kept it as a pet, which undoubtedly made the Arabs think I was a bit odd. Later another brought me an owl with an injured wing. I kept him in my tent while trying to make him better. He used to sit on my desk, but sadly one day he got into the cage and ate the jerboa.

Later the Arabs found a desert fox with his paw caught in a trap. Desert foxes are smaller than ours and a lot lighter in colour. This one had a delightful little face and lovely eyes. I got on very well with him, though he would snarl if anyone else went near him. I made a collar for him out of some cloth and a lead out of wire. We became so friendly that he would sit by me and eat from my hand. Unfortunately, he ate the owl.

One night I was woken by a scuffling and gasping noise and found that the fox had got his lead twisted around the tent rope and was choking. Half-asleep, I picked him up to unravel the lead, but in his fright he bit me on the end of the nose.

The bite was deep and the whole tip of my nose was hanging loose. I rushed back into the tent and lit a hurricane lamp to see how badly I was injured. I was the squadron's doctor as well as the commander, so I grabbed the medical kit. All I had was some old penicillin powder in small sealed bottles, which I think was supposed to be made up for injections, but I sprinkled this on and then stuck my nose up with some lint and plasters. It was stinging, but I had done all that I could.

I wasn't a pretty sight, and in the morning I told the sergeant major to give the men the day off. The Arabs were very formal and on hearing of my injury every one of them came to my tent to wish me well. It was a formality that I could have done without, sitting for half an hour saying, '*Aleikum Salaam*.'

The nose was healing but still had a dressing on when I was in my tent one morning pouring some water from a canvas water carrier into a glass and my hair suddenly bristled and stood on end, just like a dog's. It was a very strange sensation. *Oh no*, I thought, *hydrophobia!*

Fear of water is the first sign of rabies. And I knew that once the symptoms had started, there was no cure.

I was terrified, but I couldn't show it to the men, so I went out into the desert and walked and walked until I was so tired that I just collapsed. I slept for a while and when I woke up I felt all right, but I was still sure that I had rabies. I pulled myself together and thought, *Well, I'd better get through to the colonel and get a doctor.*

I got on the radio to the colonel and in a very calm and polite way told him what had happened. He understood my concern, but said that it would take four days to get a doctor out and that I would have to meet him halfway. So I had four days to carry on with my duties, knowing all the time that I was going to die from rabies.

'You cannot control your experiences, but you can control how you react to your experiences.'

I was getting pretty frightened by now because I knew that death from rabies was horrendous. I remembered my father's assistant talking about someone who had died from it and how awful it was. But I was also in command of 140 men in a desert outpost. I was the doctor, the commanding officer, everything, so I couldn't just collapse into a state of gibbering terror. That focused my mind a bit.

It was strange, really, because I was quite convinced that I was dying, and I was frightened of dying in a horrible way, but my fear of death itself didn't come up. Fear is a very strange thing. So much imagination is involved. We often fear something and when it actually happens it isn't frightening at all. Now I was faced with it, I was afraid of dying but not of death itself.

At that time I had no idea about life after death at all. That made matters even worse. How can people live, thinking that this is all that there is, that we're just chemicals that come together by accident and gain intelligence, and that one day it all just stops? It's extraordinary. But to some extent that's what I thought then. There was always a side of me that couldn't believe that that was how it was, but no one had told me anything for certain and I still hadn't found any answers for myself.

Eventually the day came for me to meet the doctor. He drove out in a Land Rover and I drove towards him and we met in the middle of the desert.

He looked at my nose and said, 'Well done. It's healing nicely. You stuck it up very well and there won't be much of a scar.'

I took a deep breath and blurted out, 'Yes, but what about rabies?'

'Oh, no chance of that. We're out of touch with diseases like that here. Animals don't contract anything, they're completely clean.'

A death sentence was lifted. I could have kissed him.

I made it up with the fox, too, but the squadron had to move to another outpost every three months and it wasn't possible to take him with me. Fortunately, the incoming captain was amused by the idea of keeping him. I thought that this was a happy ending, but I later heard that the fox bit his new owner, who promptly shot him.

I got on well with the Arabs and generally life rolled along fairly smoothly. My 140 men treated me with respect, as ordered by their sheikhs. The way of life was basic and sometimes dangerous and yet it was without pressure. I always had the feeling that if I didn't want to do something, then I needn't do it. Putting things off was the order of the day. It was an experience that was out of this world in many senses.

Not long after I left, however, oil was struck and where once we navigated sand dunes and mud flats to travel between Sharjah and Dubai, today there are modern motorways and the buzz of traffic. Sharjah and Dubai both became part of the United Arab Emirates and today are sophisticated holiday resorts.

Living with the Bedouin was an amazing experience, but my period in the desert brought me to the realization of what it meant to be in the army. I appreciated the experience I'd had, but it wasn't the way I wanted to spend my life. I was a captain at that point, in command of 140 men. If I had stayed in the army, I could have ended up being the commander of a battalion or possibly a brigade and it would just have been the same thing, only bigger – and for me a dead end. I actually saw a lot of dead-end majors and colonels. They were just ticking over. They'd gone into a cul-de-sac. I didn't want that to happen to me. At the end of my service I left the army. It wasn't for me.

What now?

Part III

On the Street

'Be resigned to the past, attend to the present and be hopeful for the future.'

CHAPTER 7

An Actor's Life...

'The soul who knows should be calm,
sure, certain that at the right time
the way will be shown.'

For two years I had lived a biblical existence. I arrived back in England totally
disorientated. In London I was completely
taken aback by the noise, the speed – the
sheer volume of everything. The people,
buildings and non-stop traffic were all overwhelming.

I quickly booked myself into a small hotel
close to Victoria coach station and stayed in
my room for two days. I didn't watch the
television and even felt hassled by the wait-
ress when she brought me a pot of tea. I
didn't want to go home or see anyone. I was
a stranger to this world and didn't like it at
all.

Eventually I rang home to say that I had
just landed and would be coming home the

following day.

I had had no leave for two years and I was entitled to extra leave because of being in the Gulf. As my army service was now finished, the War Office re-enlisted me for six months just to give me my leave entitlement. So I was out of the army, but with six months' pay.

I went to my parents' bungalow and stayed there for the whole six months, hardly ever venturing out. I spent the time building a substantial lean-to garden shed on the side of the bungalow. It survived for 40 years.

Soon my time out in the Gulf began to seem unreal, dreamlike, another world. Even now when I think back it is hard to believe that it happened. But happen it did and now it was time to face reality. What was I going to do? I had spent no money during my time in the Gulf, so I had something to live on for a while, but this wouldn't last for long.

In the meantime my father became seriously ill. He was first diagnosed with diabetes and then TB. He had never been very robust, something of a creaking gate all his life, and for a while we thought he might not survive. He had to take early retirement, but after that he rallied and fortunately was able to resume a normal life, though had to inject himself daily with insulin.

I still had an overwhelming desire to be an actor, particularly a film actor, but had no idea how to go about it. At 25 I thought that I was a bit too old for drama school.

Then I heard from a company called Oriental Carpet Manufacturers. They had been passed my name by someone I had served with in the Gulf and were looking for a person to go out to Persia, as it then was, now Iran, to buy carpets from the nomadic tribes who wove them and ship them back. Having lived rough in the desert for so long, I was seen as the ideal candidate. I would initially be employed for six months to work in the warehouse to learn about the carpets and to attend the Berlitz School of Languages to learn Persian.

I had no particular desire to do this work, but I needed to do something and it gave me the opportunity to live in London. I found a small bedsit in Earl's Court and travelled each day to the warehouse, which was by the Old Bailey.

It was interesting learning about all the different styles and weaves of Persian carpets, but to be honest it was just a job so that I could live in London for a while and sort out what to do next.

All I wanted to do was act. I didn't know why, but I felt that that was part of my destiny. I was driven to it. There was no doubt about that. I had no reservations at all apart from the fear that I might not be good enough and might not be able to get work. What if I was too shy? That was the only thing holding me back.

In fact, if I had gone straight into acting after school, I think I *would* have been too shy, too reserved. I wouldn't have made the grade, I wouldn't have been able to stand up to it. But my time in the army had given me enough confidence to have a go at it. So it had been a necessary phase. Looking back, I see that clearly.

Also, going straight from school to drama school to acting is pretty tricky, because you don't experience the real world. That can cause problems for you later.

In the meantime I was no good as a salesman. I was so unenthusiastic that one afternoon I was found asleep on a pile of rugs in the storeroom. My employers weren't pleased. And then the Persian government suddenly nationalized the carpet industry and everything changed. It was no longer necessary for me to go to Tehran. Oriental Carpet Manufacturers and I parted company, probably with relief on both sides. I could now devote myself completely to getting into acting.

I think my parents were a little worried by this, though they never said anything outright. As a good amateur actress herself, I think my mother would have been quite pleased in one sense, but she knew only too well that acting was an insecure profession. Whatever her private thoughts, however, she left me to make my own decisions.

As for my father, I remember being in the garden with him once – he was a great gardener – and I could tell he wanted to have one of those father–son conversations he thought he ought to have. But in the end all he said was, 'Are you happy with what you're doing and do you think everything will be all right?'

I said, 'I hope so.'

I certainly did.

Weekends visiting my parents were about all the social life I had at that point, though Kath and I made up for a while. In London I would spend my evenings catching up with rock 'n' roll on an old gramophone I had, and occasionally I would walk down to Earl's Court station to get some tea and sandwiches from a stall there. It was a lonely existence.

And I didn't know how to get into acting. I had no connections. I just didn't know where to start.

In desperation I took to writing to the director of every film that I went to see. I wrote very honest letters about my school acting and my experiences in the army, and got some very honest answers, often telling me that acting was a tough profession and there were plenty of experienced actors out of work. More usually, however, I was gently brushed aside with the cliché, 'We'll let you know when we have something for you.'

Nevertheless, I kept at it. Something was driving me on. I just knew that it was meant to be. I never rationalized it – at that time I never rationalized anything, really, I just got on with whatever it was I felt I wanted to do. I think at some point you do have to rationalize what you're doing, but taking highly important steps always has to be intuitive. You have to have that inner driving force. It's probably your higher self, or soul, telling you, 'This is your destiny – get on with it.' Once you've felt that, then you can start to rationalize. But if I'd started to rationalize before I went into acting, I wouldn't have done it. Getting work was so against the odds. Not that I fully realized that then – ignorance was bliss.

I was encouraged by a letter from the producer Anthony Asquith, who at the time was trying to make a film about Lawrence of Arabia. He said that when production started he was sure that there would be something for me. Sadly, production never did start until David Lean got hold of it some time later.

Then one day I received a telegram. It was from the director Brian Desmond Hurst, asking me to his mews house in Belgravia.

I was shown into a long room filled with paintings, statues and *objets d'art*. At the far end, sitting behind an ornate desk, was Brian Desmond Hurst.

'I have this letter here from you. Sit down and tell me more about yourself.'

He was a big man both physically and personally, and a very well-known director, but I felt at ease immediately and told him what he wanted to know.

When I had finished he said, 'Right.' He picked up the phone, said something softly to whoever was at the other end and then handed it to me.

'William Roache?'

'Yes, hello.'

'You're playing the part of an anaesthetist. Your call is for a week on Monday at Shepperton Studios. Will £40 a day be all right?'

That sounded wonderful to me. 'Yes.'

'It's probably three or four days' work.'

'Yes, that's fine.'

'You are a member of Equity, aren't you?'

Ah. A glorious moment came to a sudden end. In those days you couldn't work if you weren't a member of the actors' union. In spite of this I heard myself say, in a little voice, 'Yes.'

'You'll get the contract in a couple of days. Bye.'

I slowly handed the phone back to Brian Desmond Hurst, who was saying something. I wasn't really listening until I heard, 'Anyway, you've got the part. But I don't mind telling you that I'd like to go to bed with you.'

Startled, I stared at him. He had not given the appearance of being a gay man, but I suppose I was pretty naïve about such things in those days; an innocent at large you might say.

'Not now,' he said. 'I have an open house every evening and you are very welcome. You will meet some famous faces. Anyway, off you go, and if I don't see you before, I'll see you a week on Monday.'

I walked out in a daze. I'd got a film part, lied about being in Equity and been pro-positioned. I felt happy, worried and embar-rassed all at once. It was probably all in a day's work for an actor, but was I cut out for it?

Later I did go to some of Brian Desmond Hurst's parties. They were very good. I met some interesting people there. You were quite safe as long as you made sure you weren't the last to leave, and that meant not over-indulging in the Guinness and cham-pagne cocktails which were Brian's favourite tipple.

My main concern was having lied about my Equity membership. At that time the unions were paramount and members weren't allowed to work with a non-member. If I turned up, the film would be blacked. So when the contract arrived I decided to go round to the Equity office in Harley Street and own up.

*'Truth is above all else the pinnacle
to soul growth.'*

Slowly and sadly I walked into the office,

165

convinced that my first film part was going to be taken away from me.

'Well,' said the official briskly, after I had outlined the situation, 'you'd better fill in these forms. Get someone to second you and then you'll be a full member.'

I couldn't believe what I was hearing. Everyone had said that the greatest hurdle would be getting Equity membership and here I was instantly leaping that hurdle.

I know that I had lied in the first place, and that really wasn't a good thing to do, but thankfully my film part was meant to be.

'When the spirit is right,
matter will be right.'

The film was called *Behind the Mask* and starred Michael Redgrave and Tony Britton. The mask in question was a surgeon's mask – funnily enough, it was a drama about doctors. I played a young anaesthetist waiting to be interviewed for a job. I had three lines, but virtually all I had to do was walk from the waiting room through some swing doors into the interview room. The filming all went very smoothly and I will always be grateful to Brian Desmond Hurst for giving me that start, though I quickly learned not to mention his name, as the wrong conclusions would be drawn.

Meeting fellow actors was really useful, as they gave me lots of tips. One was to buy *Contacts,* a small magazine which had the names and contact numbers of all agents, film companies, casting directors and television companies.

Armed with this magazine, I set about writing even more letters, at times up to 100 a week. About half would be answered and some would lead to interviews. Quite soon I got a small part in a television series, *Ivanhoe,* starring Roger Moore who, incidentally, had also been given his big break by Brian Desmond Hurst.

Filming was taking place at Beaconsfield Studios. I was given a knitted string outfit and a balaclava, painted silver to look like armour, a bow and a quiver of arrows. Roger Moore came along and said, 'Hello.' He was looking fine in his knitted string, as he had a red tabard over it. In fact, he looked the perfect Ivanhoe except that he had curlers in his hair. He was delightful and very amusing.

I played a guard and had to look out from the battlements. To my surprise everything was shot at a terrific rate that left no time for thought or motivation. Eventually the director rushed over to me and the exchange went something like this: 'Right – Roache, is it?' 'Yes.' 'Okay, get up on the battlements there. Did you get your script?' 'Yes.' 'Well, you can forget that. I want you to look to your front, then shout over your shoulder, "My lord, a knight is coming and he rides alone," then take an arrow out of your quiver, put it in the bow, point it at the knight and then say, "Dismount, Sir Knight, and keep to the path." Have you got that?' 'I think so.' 'Right, action!'

Thinking that it was only a rehearsal, I staggered through these instructions with considerable hesitancy. But when the director said, 'Cut!' and disappeared, I realised that that was my performance and I'd barely a clue about what I was doing.

After that I got a small part in the film *The Queen's Guards*, directed by Michael Powell. Here I was a wireless operator in a tent in the desert.

My career was moving on nicely, but seeing actors at work I realized that I had a lot to learn. I thought that the only place to do this properly was in the theatre. So I started writing to theatrical companies and whenever I heard that auditions were being held for the West End I went along and read for them. One of them was for *Billy Liar* with Albert Finney. He was a very strong and likeable character, but he really made me aware of how much there was to learn. Needless to say, I did not get the part.

Around this time some people were suggesting I had started too late in the profession and should switch to something more secure. This was disheartening. Others were more encouraging, however. I started taking private lessons from a quite well-known actress called Ellen Pollack. She taught me basic stagecraft and gave me a lot of help in audition pieces. I was very grateful for her tuition.

One of the companies that I had written to was St James Management, which was run by Sir Laurence Olivier. Not having their address, I sent the letter to Olivier himself, who was playing at the Cambridge Theatre in *The Entertainer,* assuming that he would pass it on to the casting director. I was amazed when I got a short note from Sir Laurence himself, saying, 'Come to the stage door at 7.10 and I will see you for a few minutes.'

At 7 o'clock sharp I was outside the stage door. By 7.10 Sir Laurence hadn't appeared.

Oh well, I thought, *why should he remember?*

My hopes weren't very high, but nevertheless I hung on. About five minutes later he came round the corner and straight up to me.

'Mr Roache? Do come in.'

We went into his dressing room. He gave me a gin and tonic and offered me a cigarette – an Olivier, naturally – and said, 'I hope you don't mind me getting ready while we are talking.'

He sat down and started to put on his make-up, chattering away all the time about his gout and how he was going to Hollywood soon to make *The Prince and the Showgirl* with Marilyn Monroe. Here I was, a complete nobody, sitting with the world's most celebrated actor in his dressing room and feeling completely at ease. Eventually he said, 'What can I do for you?'

'Well, I've come into acting rather late,' I explained, 'and I've been told I should get out and find a more secure profession. I just thought that a word of advice from you would be worth a hundred from anybody else.'

He replied, 'Don't give up, definitely don't give up. I had two years myself that were absolutely terrible, with nothing happening at all. It was really dreadful. But if it's in you, keep at it. As I said, I'm off to America soon. When I get back, remind me about this conversation and I'll see what I can do for you.'

He shook my hand and wished me luck.

'Hope in its greatest and grandest sense illumines the way.'

I walked out full of renewed determination. I was so amazed and thrilled that such a great actor should have taken the time to be so helpful to a young unknown. Later I realized that truly great people will always find time for you and always be kind and courteous.

I didn't get in touch with Olivier in the end, as I was wary of appearing sycophantic. I wanted to make my own way. What he did for me, though, was give me new resolve. I wanted to be good, I wanted to learn, and I was sure that the only way to learn acting properly was in the theatre. So I went straight to an agent, Daphne Scorer, and said that I had been in repertory theatre in Colwyn Bay. I hadn't, of course – I'd only attended the theatre when I had been at school there – and here I was lying again, but I was getting desperate to move on and, after all, it had worked with Equity. So I decided to push my luck.

If something is meant to be, it will happen. In no time at all the agent called me in to meet Norris Staton, a producer who was looking for someone to play the juvenile lead in a summer season at Clacton-on-Sea. I sat there while she told him what a wonderful young actor I was and about all the plays that I had been in at Colwyn Bay, which was a total lie because I had never set foot on a stage in my life.

When she had finished he turned to me and said, 'If you want the job, it's yours.'

'Thank you,' I said.

We signed the contract on the spot.

The first few weeks at Clacton were hard and it was apparent that I didn't know what I was doing. At first I didn't even know the vocabulary – terms like 'upstage' and 'downstage'. A quick lesson here was: never lie beyond your own ability.

We rehearsed in the morning, then had the afternoon free and the performance in the evening. There was a lot to learn because we were doing a play a week. As I was obviously so inexperienced I was given smaller parts in the second and third plays, but I was learning fast and, with a little help from my colleagues, by the fourth play I was back to playing the juvenile lead. Donald Masters, the director, said to me, 'I've never seen anybody improve so much.' I learned a tremendous amount and will always be grateful for my time at Clacton.

I was also pleased to discover that most of my fellow actors were sensitive and insecure, rather than the outrageous extroverts I had feared. It wasn't all 'Hello, darling!' Of course there are more extrovert personalities in the profession. They tend to work in variety. But I found that most of the actors at Clacton were quite shy and acting was a way of expressing themselves.

That season also gave me my first experience of showbiz digs – and that was a bit of an eye-opener. The landlady was very strict and you had to be sat at the table on the dot for your breakfast and leave the house for the day straight afterwards. She was also very tough when it came to morals: there was one fellow in the house who was having an affair with a girl in the cast and she used to climb in through the window when they both thought everyone else was safely tucked up in bed. Anyway, the landlady's husband had a pretty shrewd idea what was going on and one night I saw him tying string outside the window with tin cans attached to it. Sure enough the girl set them off rattling on her nocturnal visit and the following morning the man was told at breakfast – in front of all of us – to pack his bags and be off. How times have changed!

I had a fling myself that summer with a young actress called Jill who fortunately had a more tolerant landlady.

Looking back on those early attempts to become an actor I am reminded of someone once asking me, 'What particular ability was it that made you want to become an actor?' and I said, 'It wasn't an ability, it was an inability, a shyness, overcoming shyness.' I think this is true for many actors. When you're on stage, you've learned your lines and you know what you're saying, so you have confidence in yourself, and the audience has to sit there and listen, and that gives you the opportunity to be something. I think it's actually childish exhibitionism that initially makes people want to become actors.

When you are working in television and films, of course, you don't get the feedback from the audience and a lot of actors will finish a scene and then turn and say, 'Was that all right?' They just want the director to say 'Well done.' At some level we're all insecure and seeking approval.

I was coming along. My aim was to do mainly theatre and to be in films occasionally. At the end of the season I went home and wrote to Nottingham Rep., which had a very good reputation and the added advantage that I could live at home. They offered me the job of assistant stage manager, which involved shifting the scenery, sweeping the stage and taking on occasional small parts, all for £6.10.0d a week. I took it because Nottingham was known for its very high standard.

This was a very different world from the summer season. It was far more serious, with some really good actors, strong direction and classical plays. It was just the place I needed to start my drama training in earnest.

There were three ASMs and one of the others was Brian Blessed. We became good friends. After seven months of hard but rewarding work I applied for an audition to Oldham Rep., which also had a good reputation. Brian helped me to choose the audition piece, from *Cat on a Hot Tin Roof*, and then coached me. It worked – I was offered the position of juvenile lead. This time I was up to the job.

I stayed at Oldham for 12 months. It was weekly rep. and I only had one play off in the whole year. The plays included *Tea and Sympathy, Meet Me by Moonlight, Charley's Aunt, A Midsummer Night's Dream, The Merchant of Venice, Night Must Fall, Of Mice and Men, The Shop at Sly Corner, Death and Brown Windsor, Robin Hood, Dinner with the Family, Goodbye, Mr Chips, Solid Gold Cadillac, The Ghost Train, Hindle Wakes, The Long and the Short and the Tall,* and many more.

By the end I was brain-numb. Performing a play in the evening, rehearsing during the day and learning lines at night was hard work. There was no time for anything else. I went to the cinema once during the year and there was not a moment without masses of learning to do, but it was the best possible drama school.

I had served my apprenticeship and now I really was an actor and ready for anything.

CHAPTER 8

Coronation Street

'There is nothing more powerful than an idea whose time has come.'

I moved back to London, took a small basement flat in Primrose Hill and started to pick up my old film contacts.

While I had been at Oldham, Granada Television had started production in nearby Manchester. I had managed to squeeze into my busy schedule the time to do one or two small parts in their drama series *Knight Errant, Biggies* and *Skyport*.

Not long after I had moved to London my agent – I was now with Terry Owen of the Lom Agency – rang to say that Granada wanted to see me about the lead in a play called *Marking Time*. It was about a young soldier stationed in Germany falling in love with a German girl. I went for the interview and was offered the part.

The play was to be broadcast as part of the

Play of the Week series. This was highly prestigious and to have the leading role was a major breakthrough. So it was that I found myself back in Manchester for the most important part in my acting career so far, one that could really establish me.

I enjoyed the play and when it was finished I went back to London to wait for it to be transmitted. I did two more small film parts, but was really waiting for *Marking Time* to be shown to kick-start my career.

While I was waiting for my big moment, my agent rang again to say that Granada wanted to see me about a serial. He thought that it was a comedy, like *Over the Garden Wall*, and it was to be called *Florizel Street.* I said that I certainly was not interested in going back to the north, as I was sure that my TV play would lead to greater things in London. But later he rang back to say that there was nothing else happening and I might as well go for the interview. So I did.

Isn't it interesting how well you do if you don't want something? There were about half a dozen people there, including the producer and casting director, but I was feeling quite relaxed, because I wasn't bothered about the part. I had the *Daily Telegraph* with me and was asked to pick an article and read it 'in Lancashire if you can'. I read an article about the Liverpool MP Bessie Braddock flicking ink pellets at a political opponent – not the most usual audition piece – and then left, not really thinking any more about it.

Then they asked if I would go up to Granada to make a pilot episode. Again I told my agent that I didn't want to do it, but he explained that it was only for three days, I would be paid and there was no other work on offer at the time. So I did the pilot, playing a university student, Ken Barlow, and again returned to London.

Granada actually made two pilots, with different casts, though some actors appeared in both. In the other, Ken was played by Philip Lowrie, who eventually played Dennis Tanner in the actual series.

I was still trying to find out the date for the transmission of *Marking Time,* as I wanted my agent to get as many directors and casting directors as possible to watch on the night.

Then he rang again, this time to say that Granada wanted me for the serial. Anticipating my refusal, he quickly went on to say that it was only going to run for 13 weeks and that he now had the transmission date for the play, which would go out right in the middle of the run.

'What a brilliant shop window,' he said. 'You're on twice a week in a serial and in the middle of its run you appear as the lead in *Play of the Week*.'

I could see the sense in this. In any case I would only have a few weeks' work after the play had been shown and offers would not come in immediately. So I agreed.

Granada decided to change the name of the serial – which was a good idea, as everyone thought it sounded like a toilet cleaner – and it was now to be called *Coronation Street;* the first episode was to be broadcast live on 9 December 1960.

All I can say is that it has been a very long 13 weeks.

This was the time of John Osborne's *Look Back in Anger*. Kitchen-sink drama. Realism. Stanislavski's method acting. James Dean and Marlon Brando. It was the beginning of the decade that burst upon the world with music, colour and new-found freedom.

Coronation Street hit the screen with the full force of that genre. It was state of the art. 'Soaps' were unheard-of at the time – we were a television drama serial and highly respected. In less than a year we were top of the ratings.

The great success took everyone by surprise. None of us knew what had hit us, not even the producer and the management. We were all instant stars, with all that entailed. And it looked set to continue. Before our 13-week run was over we had all been offered three-year contracts.

The early days were heady stuff. The cast was only 15 strong and was a close-knit community. There were some powerful characters but none more so than Violet Carson whom I insisted on calling Miss Carson out of respect for the tremendous air of authority she gave out and the fact that she was already a household name after a long run as the piano-playing Aunty Vi in Wilfred Pickles's radio show. She was like a mother to the rest of us and if anything was wrong she'd be straight up the stairs to sort it out with the management. You didn't mess with Violet Carson. What Ena Sharples was in the Street was exactly what Violet was in real life.

Then of course there were also Doris Speed and Pat Phoenix, a mix that inspired the Poet Laureate, John Betjeman, to describe the Street as Dickensian because all of the characters were strongly and clearly drawn as in all of Dickens's novels. Pat, of course, was a particularly flamboyant character in real life and was the first to go out and do personal appearances – something Miss Carson would never do – but her attempts to vie with Vi in the studio were, it has to be said, less than successful.

Tony Warren, the writer, was a man of his time and only today, nearly 50 years on, can he truly be appreciated. His scripts ranged from high drama to light-hearted comedy to powerful social documentary, all in the space of half an hour. He also established all the characters and the whole tone of the show. Many other writers came in afterwards, but he started everything off, he set the tone.

At first there were two episodes a week, at 7 o'clock on Fridays and Mondays. The Friday episode was performed live, after which there was a break and then we recorded the episode for the following Monday. In those days the recordings couldn't be edited, so doing a recording was just as stressful as doing it live. If something went wrong, we could start from the beginning again and redo it once, that's all. So Fridays were absolutely nerve-wracking. You really had to concentrate and make sure you had everything right.

Frank Pemberton, who played Ken's father, and I used to deal with the tension by rehearsing our lines in every conceivable accent. Sometimes, for a change, we would say them very quickly or very slowly – anything so that we were word perfect for the live broadcast. I remember on one occasion Frank was particularly worried about a certain word. In that scene we were sitting at the breakfast table, so he wrote it down on his boiled egg. In the heat of the moment, though, he smashed the egg before he got to that word. All I could do was watch and hope. Luckily, he got through the scene without any trouble.

We all settled into a routine. On Monday morning we had our first read-through, then in the afternoon we were given our moves for both episodes. On Tuesday morning we rehearsed the first episode and on Tuesday afternoon the second. By then we were expected to know them. I used furniture that was stored on the set for future episodes to build myself a cosy little hideaway where I could be alone until I was needed – just like the Colwyn Bay house I broke into as a schoolboy. That shyness has never really left me: I'm still not comfortable with large groups of people.

Back to the weekly routine: on Wednesday mornings we ran through both episodes again and then in the afternoon we had the technical run-through when the producer, writers, cameramen, sound engineers and other technicians came in to watch. On Thursday we went to the studio and rehearsed with the cameras and lights. At that point we talked through the episodes rather than acted them. It was done purely for the cameras. So Wednesday night was when you could go out and hit the town if you wanted, but not Thursday night, because you had to be ready for Friday, the big day. That day we would have another run-through in the morning and a full dress rehearsal in the afternoon before doing the live show and then recording the second episode.

After about three months there was a short strike by technicians, which prevented two episodes from being transmitted, and when we resumed there was no live episode. From that time onwards all of them were pre-recorded. This was a great relief, even though the method of recording still did not allow for editing or retakes, and it went on like that for the first ten years. After that they could edit a bit, though we still used to record the episodes straight through. But I think if any of them had carried on being filmed live, the show wouldn't have lasted. It would have been too much of a strain.

But the Street did continue, year after year, almost always at the top of the ratings. Through the whole of the '60s there was little change, apart from one or two new characters. The quality of the writing was extremely high and this set the standard for the direction and the acting. This consistently high quality was the reason why top actors like Lord Olivier and more recently Sir Ian McKellen wanted to appear in the show. Sadly, only Sir Ian made it; Laurence Olivier got hooked on the show when he was in hospital for a spell and they actually wrote in a part for him but his health never allowed him to take it on.

One of the reasons I was delighted with *Coronation Street* was that my family could see that I was working. You get a lot of very famous actors who are just appearing in the National Theatre or the Royal Shakespeare Company and their families never see them. But my family could see what I was doing and they were happy that I was in regular work.

Off screen, we became something of a

family too. Of course I already knew Jack Howarth, who played Albert Tatlock, from my first day at Rydal School. A long time had passed since then and Jack was now 65, but he was a stalwart professional and could always be relied on to deliver his lines perfectly. When he was telling rude stories, though, which he loved to do, he always managed to get things wrong somehow, which we all found much more amusing than the original story. I loved working with him. He was still working right up to his death at the age of 88.

Because the cast was so small and we got to know each other well, every death hit us hard. One that seemed particularly cruel was that of Graham Haberfield, who played Jerry Booth, because he was only 35 when he died of a heart attack.

Graham was a great practical joker and we were always messing around like a couple of kids. Once I was walking along a corridor when I saw him at the far end nip around a corner, ready to jump out at me. We often had mock sword fights and other tussles in the corridors and this time I thought I'd get in first. I ran quietly up the corridor and swung my foot round the corner to tap him on the leg. I did it fairly gently, but my foot met something soft and there was a huge yell. Horrified, I looked round and there was Graham. He'd been crouching down on all fours ready to jump out at me like a dog, and I'd caught him just above the eye and slit his face open.

It was Thursday afternoon and we were needed for the technical run-through, but we had to race off in a taxi to hospital instead. Meantime the rumour went round the studio that we'd had a real fight and Graham was quite badly hurt. As we were dashing into the hospital, with Graham bleeding profusely from above the eye, a woman came up to us and asked us for our autographs! Luckily, the medical staff were able to stitch him up quickly and we were even back in time for the run-through, though only just. With a bit of make-up to hide the wound, he carried on.

Things seemed to happen to Graham. In the days when each episode was shot straight through without a break, he had a scene in which he had to enter the Rover's, order a pint of beer, play the scene and at the end the stage direction was: 'He finishes his pint and leaves.' He then had to dash off behind the set to the next scene, which was a love scene with his girlfriend. In the meantime letters had been coming in saying that the head on the beer in the Rover's did not look real and the prop man had taken this very much to heart.

The dress rehearsal went well, as Graham did not actually drink the beer. When we came to do the show, he entered the Rover's, ordered a pint of beer, played the scene, finished his pint of beer and left. As he dashed off for the next scene he threw up all over the back of the set, then played the love scene with his girlfriend.

Apparently, in his eagerness to make the beer look real, the prop man had made it out of gravy browning and soda water. Never again!

As I have said, one of the more flamboyant characters in the cast was Pat Phoenix, who played Elsie Tanner. She was always lively and sparkling with energy and was an accomplished actress. Unfortunately, quite early on we clashed over how to play a scene. Ken was confronting Elsie Tanner and Ena Sharples, who had been ganging up on his wife, Val, and the idea was that they should be stunned into silence as he told them both off and then stormed out. Pat didn't think that Elsie would just stand there and take this from a young chap like

Ken and suggested that she would say, 'Oh, go on, get off!' or something like that as he made his exit. This completely ruined the dramatic moment as it had been written but unfortunately the director was influenced by Pat.

After that she had even more ideas for the scene and as we were getting ready to run through it again she came up to me and suggested that I should pause at the door so that she could pick up an ashtray and threaten to throw it at me. This was the last straw. I said, 'No, I will not. You know exactly what you have done to this scene. You are being totally unprofessional, and you know it!'

In the end the scene was neither one thing nor the other. Pat did not talk to me for two years. The feud was so subtle that I don't think that any other members of the cast were even aware of it. It was awkward, though, and I'm glad to say that finally we did make it up. On her birthday one year she decided to hold a party at her house. She had invited the whole cast apart from me, but that afternoon we were shooting a scene together and as we were waiting to go into the Rover's, she said, without looking at me, 'If you want, you can come tonight.'

'Thank you, Pat,' I replied.

That night at the party we talked a lot and got on well. The incident was never mentioned again and we put it behind us. As time went on we gained a lot of respect for each other and in later years, when Pat became interested in spiritual matters and joined the Rosicrucians (a mystical organisation named after the Rosy Cross, which you can follow on the Internet or by post) she would come to talk to me almost every day. I really enjoyed these discussions and they went on until she left the show. Then she lost interest in the Rosicrucians and took up with politics via her relationship with Cherie Blair's father, the actor Tony Booth.

I always had quite a serious attitude towards things and this came out in the early days of the show when we started a poker school. I couldn't just go and chuck some money in and have a bit of fun, as some people did; I had to get books on the game and really work on it. I even had a special bag of money that was my poker money, and if I was ever down at the end of the week I was really cross with myself. In the end I actually got quite good and so did Alan Rothwell, who played my brother. We thought we were so good that we went along to a professional poker school at a club in Manchester, the Cabaret Club, to watch the games. One Saturday night I was determined to sit in. I took along £60, which was quite a lot of money in those days, and ended up playing with a silent trio of professional gamblers. I was out of my depth and I knew it. Poker is a game of percentages and you learn to make the best of a good hand; fortunately, I had one really good hand and managed to leave the table in the early hours of the morning with exactly the same amount of money that I'd arrived with. But I felt absolutely drained. That was enough for me. After that I lost the desire to play, but learned the lesson that if you must play, make sure that you play with people of your own level.

Later, the cast moved on to play bridge. I found that very enjoyable and became a good instant teacher of the game.

A system for generating the storylines was established fairly early on and, broadly speaking, it is still followed today. About 14 writers, about three or four script editors and a producer form a storyline committee and create the overall storylines for the next three months. Then the script editors break those down into episodes and each episode is handed to one of the writers to put the dialogue in. So those who do the dialogue have been involved in the creation of the storyline and no single writer is ever responsible for the overall continuity. It's a very good system. To ensure continuity there is also a 'bible', listing all the characters' past histories.

As time passed by, playing Ken became second nature to me. When you're on the stage, going from play to play, you have to understand a new character all the time and then take that character through a set of circumstances. Actors in a serial have to take their character through many different sets of circumstances. Working on *Coronation Street* for so long, I obviously got to know Ken really well.

Also, *Coronation Street* was always character-based rather than story-based. That was one of its strengths. So people knew, more or less, how the characters were going to react. Ken was the intellectual, the university graduate from within the street, and there was a time when the writers used to portray him as intellectually arrogant and a bit pompous. He was a schoolteacher and

My parents, William and Hester Roache, pictured during the early years of their married life.

Rutland House, my birthplace in Ilkeston, Derbyshire.

With Beryl, 1934. My swimsuit was probably a hand-me-down from my sister!

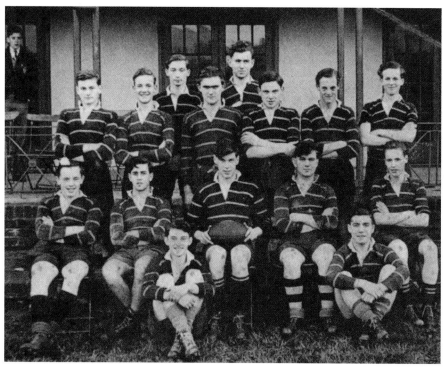

A proud member of the First XV rugby team at Rydal Senior School, Colwyn Bay, in 1946. I am sitting on the far right.

Me, at sixteen, in the garden of Rutland House with Patch, the dog.

The Royal Welch Fusiliers cricket team in Kingston, Jamaica, 1953. I'm second from the right, with Major Tolhurst on my right.

At the fort in the Buriemi Oasis in Trucial Oman. Note the dashing moustache.

Aged twenty-six, and just embarking on a career in acting.

The cast of *Coronation Street* as of episode one, December 1960. *Back row, left to right:* Harry Hewitt (Ivan Beavis), Albert Tatlock (Jack Howarth), Ivan Cheveski (Ernst Walder), Dennis Tanner (Philip Lowrie), David Barlow (Alan Rothwell), Jack Walker (Arthur Leslie), an unnamed extra (William Croasdale), Frank Barlow (Frank Pemberton), Ida Barlow (Noel Dyson), Minnie Caldwell (Margot Bryant).
Front Row: Annie Walker (Doris Speed), Florrie Lindley (Betty Alberge), Linda Cheveski (Anne Cunningham), Elsie Tanner (Patricia Phoenix), Ena Sharples (Violet Carson), Christine Hardman (Christine Hargreaves), Kenneth Barlow (William Roache), an extra (Patricia Shakesby), an extra (Penny Davies), Martha Longhurst (Lynne Carol).

The five longest-running cast members celebrate the Street's eighteenth birthday in 1978. Jack Howarth, Doris Speed, Pat Phoenix, Violet Carson and I toast the future.

The turnout for Ken and Deirdre's screen wedding in 1981.

Doorstep confrontation: Ken and Mike shape up for one of the most gripping half hours in British television.

Will it be happily ever after for Wendy Crozier (played by Roberta Kerr) and Ken? In the end it was Wendy, not Mike, who led to the Barlow marriage breakup.

The Street's line-up in 1992, with the cast now well into three generations.

Coronation Street fan John Betjeman visits Granada Studios, Sadly, he never realised his ambition to appear in the programme.

The Queen and Prince Philip open Granada's new purpose-built Street set. Her Majesty became so engrossed in chatting to us all that the visit overran by half an hour.

Is Mike Baldwin about to clock Ken? Deadly rivals on-screen, in real life Johnny Briggs and I are the best of friends.

Dancing with Mary Healey in the play *Lighthearted Intercourse* at the Liverpool Playhouse, directed by Anthony Tuckey, 1971.

Another great golf day at Turnberry in 1983, with Gary Player, Peter Alliss, Terry Wogan and Tony Jacklyn. Sara was caddying for me in a matching outfit.

Celebrating summer solstice with the Druid Order at Stonehenge.

Margaret and Denis Thatcher welcome us to Downing Street shortly after the 1983 general election.

Sara and I were delighted when Betty Driver agreed to be our daughter Edwina's godmother. Here we are at the christening, with Verity and her godmother, Eileen Derbyshire.

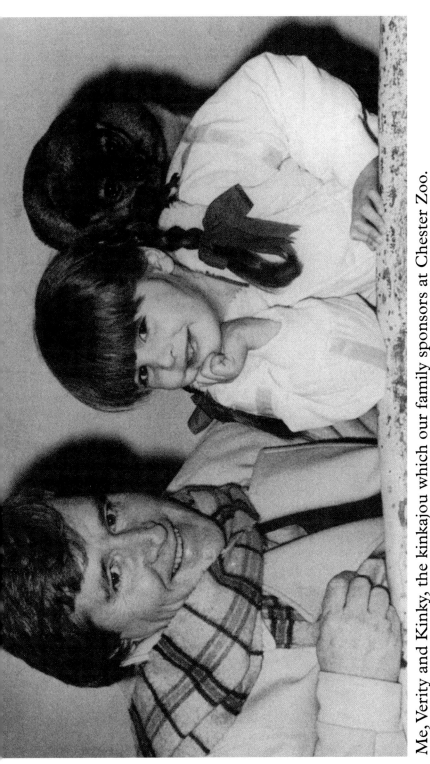

Me, Verity and Kinky, the kinkajou which our family sponsors at Chester Zoo.

Posing for a portrait by renowned artist John Bratby R.A.

As a second lieutenant during Her Majesty's visit to Kingston, Jamaica in 1953.

Captain Roache with a group of young trainees for the Trucial Oman Scouts, Sharjah 1955.

With Sara, announcing our engagement in 1976 — as you can see from the prominent ring!

With Sara on our wedding day, 3rd July 1978, looking forward to being one of showbusiness's most enduring marriages.

My parent's celebrating their 75th birthdays in 1975, as they were both born in 1900.

Celebrating *Coronation Street's* 30th anniversary with Les Dawson, his wife, Sara and Ivan Beavis.

The family, with Sara, Verity and Edwina in 1983, not long before we were to lose her.

Peggy Kennard at her home in 2004, shortly before her death.

Selwyn Hughes on a brief visit to Granda in 1996, the last time I saw him.

With Sara at Buckingham Palace after receiving my MBE from the Queen in 2000.

Meeting Prince Charles at Highgrove in 1999 — I didn't remind him that Ken and Deirdre had married on almost the same day he had married Princess Diana, as Camilla was standing nearby!

A bit of fun with Ian McKellan when he joined the cast in 2004, with Will and Sara.

On one of Linus's visits from America, with Will, Christmas 2003.

A family group after doing *Star Lives*, with Verity, Sara and Will.

he was living a very proper and upright life – well, some of the time! I wasn't like him – I'm from a middle-class background and Ken isn't, I'll have a go at most things but Ken wouldn't. Fortunately, all I had to do was like him, understand him, believe him and, as I've said, take him through the circumstances that were written for him. And that was fine. That I could do.

In the early days a lot of people used to confuse me with Ken, however. At that time we weren't allowed to give interviews or appear on celebrity talent shows or variety shows and so on, so people couldn't see what we were really like and often believed we were like our characters. Now those rules are much more relaxed and there are so many behind-the-scenes features anyway that it's less of a problem. But it does seem that people will always believe that if you're playing someone there must be a bit of them in you.

In a way, there was, because later on Ken played the trumpet. The first occasion was at a Christmas concert at Ena Sharples's mission hall and the second was when Ernie Bishop (Stephen Hancock) formed a band. It consisted of Ernie on piano, Billy Walker (Ken Farrington) and me on trumpet and

Alan Howard (Alan Browning) on the guitar. We played 'Yellow Bird' in front of 16 million people. But I have to admit, I played as badly as ever.

Years later Tony Warren told me how I had landed the part of Ken. Apparently he had seen me when I was recording *Marking Time* and had brought the casting director, Jose Scott, out to see me. Their minds were made up on the spot.

I was very grateful for it. Suddenly I was famous, fêted and wanted for personal appearances. People wanted my opinions, I could get tables in restaurants and all sorts of invitations came my way. There were lots of advantages and almost a feeling of safety in being well known. Initially it was highly enjoyable.

Everything seemed to be going very well. The year after *Coronation Street* was first broadcast I married the actress Anna Cropper, whom I had met at Nottingham Rep., and over the next few years we had two children, Linus and Vanya. She was a great person who also had a wonderful warmth and beauty in her acting and for a time it was a good marriage. We had a four-storey Queen Anne house next to Camden Passage in Islington (for which I paid the then magnificent sum of £12,000!), and a cottage in Rawtenstall, to the north of Manchester. As I wasn't sure how long *Coronation Street* was going to continue, I wanted to keep a London base. My family lived there and I went back there for weekends and spent the weeks in the north.

Fame is a strong test of character, though, and any weaknesses will manifest. You have money and opportunity, so you soon find out who you really are. Perhaps it went to my head. It was the '60s, freedom and experimentation were in the air, and I started living the high life. Fortunately drugs were never attractive to me, but I drank quite a lot. Apart from the hangovers, it was not a problem and was not out of control, but although it never interfered with my work, I was drinking more than was good for me.

Also, I was misbehaving with the girls – there was a different one each week. This is not something I am proud of. I like to think of myself as a responsible person, but I wasn't behaving responsibly back then. I had the security of family life but also the opportunity to live the life of a bachelor, and I took it. I knew I was letting myself and my family down and I felt guilty, but still I carried on. I didn't seem to have any control over myself.

I didn't go to pubs but if I was taking a girl out I'd start with a couple of gin and tonics, have a bottle of wine over dinner and a brandy afterwards. I rarely went to parties because I could never hear what people were saying, but when I did I'd be there until four in the morning and it doesn't pay in my line of work to turn up with red eyes. Despite the fact that I never had an alcoholic blackout, there came a time when I realized that this sort of behaviour had to stop.

'The government of your life is a matter that lies entirely between God and yourself, and when your life is swayed and influenced from any other source you are on the wrong path.'

On the surface I had everything anyone could want. *Coronation Street* was more popular than ever. I was also able to take time out to do some theatre work – Richard Gordon's *Doctor in Love* at the Alhambra Theatre, Bradford, and John Bowen's *Disorderly Women* in Manchester and London – and received some very good reviews. I was famous, had some money, the obligatory flash sports car and was free to do whatever I wanted. I should have been happy, but I was not. In fact I felt completely lost.

Whether my state of mind had anything to do with it or not I don't know, but it was around this time that I had an unnerving experience at our house in Islington. In a spirit of experimentation, we decided to have a table-rapping session one evening with a group of friends. We wrote out the alphabet and the words 'yes' and 'no' on scraps of paper and laid them out in a circle on the table. Then, each placing a finger on the bottom of an upturned wine glass in the centre of the circle, we asked if anyone was there.

The glass started to move very positively and to give clear messages. After a while it became more energetic and started to spell out 'Kill,' 'Kill,' 'Kill.' The speed and strength of the movement were alarming.

After this had gone on for a few moments we asked if anyone was there.

'Yes.'

With amazing clarity we were told that it was a man who had lived in the attic of the house. He had been an ostler (the man who looked after the horses in the days before motor cars) and had been unfaithful to his wife, who had found out and murdered him.

Suddenly the glass rushed around again, spelling, 'Kill her,' 'Kill her.'

We were really getting quite frightened by now, but then one foolhardy participant took it further.

'Can you appear?'

'Yes,' came the answer, to our great alarm.

'When?'

'At midnight.'

At that some of us wanted to stop. But my friend persevered.

'Where?'

'In the mirror in the hall.'

That was it. We all stopped and most of the company made a hasty departure. Of those who were left, none went into the hall at midnight, or at all that night. It was a scary experience and not one I would wish to repeat because the entities that are around are the astral-stuck ones looking for opportunities to get in and you've got idiots and bad people there just as you've got anywhere else. You are not going to be getting your angel or your high being on that level, you are only going to attract the lower entities and, believe me, that's not good. Such beings are earth-bound spirits who can be vicious and who refuse to ask for the help that is readily available to them. You can get some information from them but it's not reliable and you open up a channel which is best not opened.

After this the atmosphere changed in the house and it felt much less friendly. The cleaner refused to go into the top flat, which had been the attic. A dog that was visiting the house wouldn't go into that flat either. We left soon after that. The move had already been arranged, but I was glad to go.

If you want proof of the existence of other realms, don't try it yourself, as we did. Go to a Spiritualist church. Or, better still, if you want to find out more about spiritual matters, ask your higher self for understanding and see what comes along. Your higher self is always there and you only need to ask – in your mind, don't speak it – especially before you go to sleep at night. Those thoughts have energy, those thoughts are listened to, it is true prayer. Every thought that is asking for understanding is answered: your higher being will find a way of getting that answer to you – it may come as a dream, as a thought that comes into your mind, a chance meeting. Remember, there is no such thing as coincidence. It's also worth knowing that in the next world there are houses, schools and universities – even concerts. It's just as real as here. What we refer to as dying is really going home. Where we are now is quite a frightening place. Thank God it's only temporary. If only I had known all this then, but the simple fact is I did not. I didn't have a clue. Material success had not brought me happiness – in fact it had made me realize the true emptiness of my life. By the time *Coronation Street* had been running for ten years, I was at my lowest point. I had never felt so depleted. Indulging my appetites had not satisfied me, but drained me physically, emotionally and mentally.

I was still afraid of death and infinity and could take no comfort in what the Church had to offer. I knew that there had to be more to life than this, but what was it? Where was it? How was I ever going to find it?

CHAPTER 9

The Master

'When the pupil is ready...'

The dream was vivid and full of detail. I was in the ramshackle study of Thomas Maugham, a homeopathic doctor I had met just a week or so earlier at his home in south London. He was seated behind his large roll-top desk surrounded by endless books and papers, just as he had been when I first made his acquaintance. He leaned forward, looked at me closely and said, 'Why don't you come and join us, Bill?'

That was all that happened, but the dream was so clear, it stayed with me. I was baffled; quite frankly, I had no idea what to make of it.

The following day I had an appointment to see Dr Maugham in his homeopathic capacity. As I walked into that study he looked at me just as he had in the dream, that half-smile on his face, and said in the calm and rational voice I was to come to know so well, 'Did you get my message, Bill?'

'Yes,' I heard myself reply somewhat feebly.

Then, very simply, Dr Maugham said – much as he had in my dream – 'You're very welcome to come and join us, Bill.'

I was stunned. I felt a tingling in my spine. I could hardly believe what I'd just heard. It was absolute evidence to me that things happen on a higher plane beyond our five senses. I was tremendously excited to have experienced something so wonderful. He and I had no discussion about it: we both just knew. That was perhaps the greatest experience of my life – a truly life-changing experience. It moved my understanding up into a higher level and took away all my doubts and fears.

'Miracles are not contrary to nature, only contrary to what we know about nature.'

And that was how Thomas Maugham – a man I now refer to as The Master – came into my life in such a powerful way. Some time earlier I had been talking to a friend about how low I was feeling and she told me about this homoeopathic doctor who lived in Dulwich – Dr Maugham. She said that he was an unusual man and was rumoured to be more than just a doctor. She gave me his number and I made an appointment to see him.

His home was a modest private house in a tree-lined road. I rang the bell and the door was opened by an attractive woman who smiled and ushered me into the waiting room. It was quite large, with long benches placed against the walls and in three rows in the middle of the room. I thought that it seemed somewhat excessive for a doctor's practice.

After a while the woman said the doctor would see me and asked me to go up the stairs, where I would find his study – 'It's the room with the door open.'

I duly went up the stairs, through the open door and into one of the most untidy rooms I had ever seen. There were, as I've said, piles of books and papers against the walls and on the left hand side a small curtained area, which I subsequently learned was where the doctor kept his homoeopathic remedies.

Dominating the room was that large roll-top desk, behind which sat a most extraordinary man. He was small, bald and wiry, with a long grey beard and the darkest brown eyes imaginable. Though elderly, he seemed strangely ageless. I had been told that he was in his 90s, but if it had been said that he was 60 or 200 years old, either would have been believable. This was Dr Maugham.

As I walked towards him his look was penetrating yet gentle. I had the peculiar feeling that he could see into my very soul.

He motioned me to sit down in a chair next to the desk and said in a good clear voice, 'Why have you come here?'

'I feel empty – depleted physically, mentally and spiritually,' I replied.

He stared at me for some considerable time. This should have been unnerving, but it wasn't. I felt comfortable with him and very safe. Then he stood up and went behind the curtained area, emerging a few minutes later with a small brown bottle from which he tapped a pill into my hand and told me to dissolve it slowly under my tongue before tapping others into a brown envelope to take away. These were homeopathic remedies (never to be touched by another's hands) of which I have since become a staunch advocate.

'Take one of these tonight, one tomorrow morning and one tomorrow night,' he said.

'They will make you feel better.'

Then he added, 'I have meetings in my waiting room every other Thursday at seven. Why don't you come along?'

'Thank you, I will,' I replied. Looking back I can see I was being guided, though I had no idea at the time why I was willing to be so compliant.

I left, but his presence stayed with me for a long time.

The following Thursday I went along to the meeting. The waiting room was packed and people were spilling out into the hall. There must have been 50 or 60 there. I noticed that they were all about my age or younger. Most of them seemed to know each other and were chattering away. Some appeared to be in charge of the arrangements and one of them beckoned me to a space on one of the benches.

Suddenly, for no apparent reason, the room fell silent. Then, after a few seconds, the doctor walked in. He walked up to a chair and small table placed at the head of the room, looked around, smiled and started talking.

His words were like drops of water in an oasis. Here were the things that I had waited all my life to hear. Whatever he said, I knew,

I just knew, that he was speaking the truth.

When he finished there was a group meditation. He started by asking us all to visualize a large circle of light around the whole room for protection, then to sit up straight, balance our breathing, concentrate on the centre of our brow and imagine it was a lovely day and we were sitting on a log in a forest clearing.

There was a wonderfully peaceful silence for the next 20 minutes. Dr Maugham ended it by saying, 'Has anyone anything to report?' I wondered what he meant, but then the reports came flooding in. People described what they had seen or where they had been and every time the doctor would explain it to them. It was truly fascinating.

Then he invited questions. There was not one he could not answer. Sometimes, though, he would tell the questioners something about themselves rather than answer the question directly. With one girl he was surprisingly severe, but she thanked him profusely when he had finished. With his abruptness Dr Maugham had shown her that there was no point in constantly falling away from the beliefs and coming back. Her erratic behaviour was her enemy.

At the end of the meeting, his parting

words were, 'Enjoy yourselves.'

I went home with a lot to think about. Things that he had said would suddenly pop into my mind and I felt great enjoyment in thinking about them. He was moving my understanding forward.

Then came the dream that was to bind me to Dr Maugham for the rest of his days.

Dr Maugham truly was a master. He was aware of things beyond the span of our finite minds. Whereas so many cult leaders just want your money, he just wanted you to grow, get out there in the world and do your thing, whatever that was. When he looked at someone, he saw their state of being. I had arrived in a pretty depraved state and once, after a few meetings with him, made the mistake of asking him a thoughtless question.

'How are you?' I said.

He looked at me, then said levelly, 'A lot better than you.'

How right he was. In me he could see the effects of years of indulgence. I wasn't too impressed at the time, of course, but looking back, it was just what I needed.

'Your worth is what you are,
not what you know.'

207

Dr Maugham appeared at the right time for me. They do say that the master appears when the pupil is ready. You can't go looking; it's no good rushing around saying, 'I want this and I want that and why haven't I got a master?' Whatever you need will be presented to you when you are ready. It might not be a master, it might come in some other form, but if you open yourself up to the idea and genuinely want to move forward, everything that you need will be given to you. Often you won't realize it at the time, and I didn't really, but now I know that's how it works. When you're ready, you will find whatever you need.

'Truth is not acquired, but discovered.'

When I met Dr Maugham I was ready to receive, and I got what I wanted. I just soaked it all up. I absorbed it all and have continued to do so ever since.

I grew to love that man and, if he had allowed it, would have grown to depend on him. But he wanted everyone he taught to stand on their own two feet. He wanted us to work on our own selves and to move forward independently. Ultimately, he wanted us to realize our oneness with God. He wanted us to be masters.

So many cults have a personality at the head and try to draw people in. Here there was none of that. No money was asked for, though you did have to have commitment. If you didn't keep up to the mark, you would be asked to leave. Dr Maugham was a no-nonsense teacher, but it was clear that he wanted the best for us – he wanted us to get up to his standard and go beyond it.

Until I met him I had no spiritual focus whatsoever. I had been to the meeting at the Spiritualist church and witnessed something that intrigued me, but not taken it further. I had read my daily horoscope, but had never learned any more about astrology. I had seen the strange figure and the blue Buddha at Rutland House, but not even told anyone about them. I had experienced the spirit communication in the Islington house, but been frightened by it. Whenever anyone had a tale to tell about something out of the ordinary, I was interested in it, but there was no focus to my enquiries, no direction, and I still thought that the Church was the authority on spiritual matters, even though its answers didn't satisfy me. My own life didn't satisfy me either. I was ready to listen to the doctor and to study under him. I was ready to learn. It was a great turning point in my life.

I studied under the doctor until his death some four years later. He would hold public meetings, which were always packed out, and then we would be broken down into groups for further study. I started off in a group of about ten people, then one or two dropped out. We were all fairly similar; there might have been differences in education and background, but there was definitely a strong sense of togetherness, a tremendous fellow feeling. We were all at the same level on the same search, on the steep path of self-evolvement. It was wonderful to know that I wasn't alone. Furthermore, I was not handicapped by being a celebrity; in fact, I was pitied for it because the others knew that I had extra work to do on getting rid of the ego that holds us back spiritually. At one stage I even considered giving up my job for that very reason.

'Put all wishes aside save the one desire to know the truth. Then act upon it immediately it is revealed.'

Although we were in groups, the focus was more on individual evolvement than learning as a group or learning from the group. It was all very much about personal understanding and personal responsibility. There was no rigid scheme of learning and no qualifications. All Dr Maugham did, in fact, was open us up to the truth that we are all eternal beings. He explained that the whole point of being here is to develop spiritually and then to be of service to others, to help others as best you can. Basically, that's all it was. It was wonderfully simple.

I have had one contact with him since he passed. I don't normally go to mediums but on one occasion both my wife Sara and I went to see one and she told me she had a very strong person coming through from the Other Side who said, 'Who's wearing the trousers in your house?' I knew not only that it was Dr Maugham but also what he was referring to: Sara is a very strong person – exactly what I always needed.

For Dr Maugham, coming back like that is a sacrifice for the high spiritual being. They have to re-enter the lower vibrations and that isn't pleasant. The great ones – just like all of us – are constantly moving onwards and upwards, so their return always marks a great sacrifice. Jesus Christ was the ultimate example of this; he was a master who decided to come back to teach us to love one another. He was the greatest and most highly evolved being ever to make the ultimate sacrifice to reincarnate. He's still up there, going ever higher. He still cares about humanity on earth and he's walking the spiritual realms as we speak, very much a living being.

'We are all gods in the making.'

Dr Maugham was head of the Ancient Order of Druids, an ancient esoteric school, but their fundamental teaching has always been to search for the truth, so although the Druid Order was an initial focus for me, it was really just the beginning. It introduced me to many new ideas, but it also taught me to go out and look at other schools like Hinduism, Buddhism and Theosophy. The trouble was that the media picked up on the druidry and got pictures of me going round Stonehenge and that was it: 'He's a druid!' I was pigeonholed and that can be a great disadvantage because if you say you are anything some people will not like what you are. This was the other side of fame – you could be subject to intense media scrutiny at times and it wasn't pleasant. People would also tend to label you, not always accurately, and I find that labels are counterproductive – in fact actually harmful, because when people put you in a category they restrict you and some will judge you or dislike you for it.

Ironically, the whole point of the druid philosophy is to search for the truth in your own way. You're not indoctrinated when you're studying with them; in fact, you're taught to break down your opinions and have a good old look at everything. They will present you with certain ideas, but if you don't like what they're teaching, that's fine, you just leave it. And then off you go, on your own, and start to plough your own furrow and follow your own interests and instincts. That's what happened to me. I don't subscribe to any religion or philosophy. I'm not part of any cult. I'm just searching for the truth.

That sounds simple, but it is the hardest thing of all, because to do it properly you have to examine your opinions, your beliefs, your assumptions – everything you've been brought up with. You have to lay everything on the ground, open yourself up and virtually start again. But I was very fortunate in that I had Dr Maugham to help me do it.

I know very little of his background. Nobody knew anything, really. We didn't need to know. I didn't need to know. It was irrelevant. We knew he was a master by what he said to us. I never heard him say anything that was not totally true. And in his company you yourself always had to be frank and truthful. He would know if you weren't. He never became angry, but I did witness him lashing someone with the tongue of severity because it was needed.

Although he was our teacher, it wasn't like a traditional school at all. The trouble with schools is that they are like sausage machines, injecting information into people and then throwing them out. What they should do is to take each individual and look at them and develop their particular aptitudes, skills and interests. Dr Maugham did this with each one of us. I remember going to him once with a problem and he said, 'Just forget everything. Now instinctively, what do you feel you want to do? What insight comes to you?' And suddenly I realized I could answer my own questions. So I learned that if you can pose a question correctly, you've usually arrived at the answer. Of course, the trick is posing the question!

One way of doing this is through meditation. That was one of the first things Dr Maugham taught us. Meditation is essential to spiritual development. It can also help with all other aspects of life. At the lowest level it can reduce stress, anxiety, tension and worry. At the highest level it enables you to tune in to your soul. The main purpose of meditation is to quieten the mental, emotional and physical aspects of oneself, thus allowing a greater contact with the higher, or spiritual, self.

'Meditation is the clarifier
of a beclouded mind.'

There are some golden rules for meditation. It is important to find a quiet place where you feel calm and peaceful and are safe from interruption. This place will become even more calm and peaceful as you progress because it will take on the aura of your meditation.

Then you must find that all-important chair. It must be comfortable yet firm and upright and your feet must touch the floor without any undue pressure under the knees. Some time and thought need to be taken over these first two steps.

Then select a time of day. If it is possible, try to make it the same time each day. The more this becomes a set routine, the better. If your lifestyle will not allow this (mine rarely does), don't despair. Just finding a little time to sit quietly, wherever you are, will still be good.

Having found the place, chair and time, the next stage is to prepare yourself. As you walk into the room, leave all thoughts of daily life outside the door. You can pick them up later.

*'Enter into thine inner chamber
and shut the door.'*

The first requirement in meditation is discipline of the mind, emotions and body. This will take time. It can be very frustrating at the beginning, but you must guard against impatience. Do not expect immediate results, but keep at it and you will have the most glorious reward. Initially 20 minutes is enough time, or even less.

Sit upright with your feet squarely on the floor and your hands resting gently on your legs. Ensure that you have no tight clothing and nothing is restricting the body. Spend some time making sure you are comfortable. This is the first of the disciplines – keeping the body relaxed but alert.

Now imagine that your consciousness is residing in the centre of your brow. Hindus often have a mark in this area. Sit quietly and concentrate your thoughts on the brow's centre.

Now balance your breathing. Make sure it is even – not too deep or too long. Breathe in for the same length of time as you breathe out. Imagine waves on the seashore gently coming in and then going out.

You are now meditating.

If any distracting thoughts come, let them come in and then go back out. You will find that the body will try to distract you with physical discomfort and the mind will keep wanting to think about a whole variety of things. All sorts of emotions will start playing tricks with you. Keep at it! Don't let anything deflect you from your purpose. Each session will get better as you learn to recognize where the distraction is coming from and then deal with it. There's no need to be impatient. Impatience is itself a distraction.

As you begin to get control, you can

introduce some exercises. Think of a circle of light around you like a big hoola-hoop. Keep it going in an anti-clockwise direction. Make it bright and build it so that it stays with you. This will give you protection.

If any other lights or visions appear, just observe them. You may see some startling things, but simply be detached and observe. Don't be afraid, particularly if your circle of light is shining. You can ask for help and protection, but always try to remain the observer. Once you are quiet and stand back, your higher self, or soul, can come in and communicate with you.

When you are sufficiently in control you can start to visualize places. You might like to imagine you are in a beautiful country place that you know or somewhere by the sea. Try to visualize it accurately and place yourself there. You may see someone else there, someone perhaps you can talk to. But don't be disappointed if nothing happens. Don't have any expectations, just observe.

When I first started meditating, it was very frustrating. I was amazed to find how angry I felt. I didn't think I was angry, but an anger would come. I was angry with myself – annoyed by my inability to be totally calm and peaceful and controlled. I thought I should be able to be like that, but I was restless. But after a while I would get to the point where I could calm down and I would feel very peaceful. Sometimes I'd meditate for about two hours. I found it was a great help to me, especially when it made me realise that there was some irritation and a bit of anger there.

Some people think meditation is sitting down and thinking about something, taking a subject – the meaning of life, or God, or whatever – and thinking about that. I never meditated with a project, as it were, or a thought to develop. I just wanted to surrender the lower self and let the higher come in.

We started off meditating in small groups. But the most important meditations were always the ones that we did on our own.

When I first started meditating I used to think that with the correct technique I could achieve instant enlightenment by raising the kundalini, the life force that is based at the bottom of the spine. When this force is raised it travels up through the chakras, the seven sacred energy centres, and eventually connects the pituitary and pineal glands and brings you to a higher level of consciousness. It has tremendous power and can only be raised when you are able to control it and are ready for the subsequent contact with the higher source.

I tried desperately to raise this force on one occasion. It resulted in a blinding flash in my head and I passed out. I was unconscious for some minutes. I did not try it again, but since then have worked steadily to get myself to a state of preparedness when it will happen naturally and easily.

Spiritual development is a slow process and you can only move forward when you're ready. You can't just sit down and decide to make great advances through meditation, however intensely you try that. You can't do it through effort of will. It took me a while to find that out. Eventually I realized you enlighten yourself by *becoming* a better person, an enlightened person.

Meditation is of course an important part of this process, because it is basically a way to relax and let the higher self come in and inspire you. It might not come during the meditation but later, when you're doing other things. That's fine.

'It is through your own soul that the voice of God speaks to you.'

Ultimately, the aim is to be meditating at some level all the time, whether you're doing the washing up or are out walking or whatever. That way, at any given moment you will be able to go into a more intense state of deep inner peace. You will also have a continual connection to your higher self and access to great wisdom.

After a while I did feel that I was making progress with this. I would have phases of meditating very deeply and really feeling that I was benefiting from it. And then for some reason it would stop and I wouldn't meditate at all for quite a while. Then I'd come back to it and sometimes I'd find that unconsciously it had carried on and I had improved. But at other times I'd feel all the old irritation again and be upset that I wasn't getting anywhere.

I realized that it was very easy to be swept along by day-to-day things and get caught up in all the hurly-burly of life and lose any inner tranquillity that I had achieved. When I first started meditating, there was quite a lot of turbulence in my life. Whenever there was a crisis it would be harder to meditate, but I knew the importance of it during those times, so I made a greater effort to do so and I think I did get more benefit from it then.

If ever you have gone through a period of not meditating and feel you've fallen right back, look at where you've fallen back to and where you used to fall back to in the past and you will see that you have progressed. Life always moves forward. The life force itself is a progressive thing and we are part of that. We cannot stand still – whether we want to or not. So even if you think you're not moving forward, you are. Even when you think you're standing still, life is nudging you forward.

CHAPTER 10

Thinking Things Through

'The more you believe, the less you know.'

One thing that Dr Maugham told us was to think things through. This might sound obvious to some, but it was a revelation to me. Until that time I had never thought anything through. I had never thought through the army, I had never thought through any of my paranormal experiences, I had never thought through the fame and fortune, the life I was leading – I had just accepted whatever came to me and carried on.

During the '60s everything had been opening up. Everything had been up for grabs, as it were. After the austerity of the war years and the post-war years, suddenly there had been a lot more freedom – financial freedom, sexual freedom, freedom in thinking. And in some ways I had been of the time, and had enjoyed those freedoms, but my thinking had not developed. At a fundamental level I had always wanted to get to the heart of what life and death were all about, but I hadn't done anything about it. Now I felt that at last I was taking the first steps on a journey of understanding. After meeting Dr Maugham I finally started to think things through.

'The moment we fully and vitally realize who and what we are, we begin to build our own world, even as God builds His.'

To do this properly, of course, you have to be aware of who you are and where you are and what is going on around you. One of the little exercises Dr Maugham set us was to spend a day watching ourselves, being an impartial observer in our own lives, just listening to what we said and what others said to us and seeing what happened to us. That was fascinating to do. When you become an independent observer, you realize that you often change when you're with different people, become somebody else. You realize how much prattle and inconsequential chatter is part of your daily routine. How much of your life is unthinking habit. How much is absolutely automatic: get up, clean your teeth, get dressed, get in the car, go to work, have coffee, lunch, afternoon tea... How often do you make a conscious decision before you do anything? In my case, it was very, very rarely.

As you become an observer of your own life, you also become self-aware. You may see aspects of yourself that you don't like, aspects that are really crude. Then you can gently start to improve on those areas, maybe by swearing a bit less and drinking a bit less or whatever. There's no need to do this harshly – you don't need to wear a hairshirt or anything. Simple measures will be effective. And as you carry them out, you will find that you become even more self-aware. It is an ongoing process of self-improvement and in time it becomes part of you – you don't even think about it, but it's there, built in.

And then you learn the truth of something else that Dr Maugham taught, which was: 'You yourself are the greatest hindrance to finding the truth.'

This might sound paradoxical – if we are the ones looking for the truth, how can we be our greatest hindrance? The reason is that our opinions and beliefs can often get in our way. We all tend to take beliefs and absorb them into our understanding of reality so that they become unconscious and we barely realize that we have them, let alone that they are just beliefs, not the truth. So unconscious beliefs can hinder our development – they are something that has been instilled in us, they are stepping stones but at some point in our lives they need to be challenged. In order to overcome this problem, we first have to become aware of what they are, to make them conscious. Then we can examine them and the role they play in our lives and see whether they are serving us or not. So again we have to gain greater awareness. Awareness is the key to everything and that means we should always be ready to change.

As we become more aware, we may not only see our beliefs for what they are, but even discard them. Beliefs can be stepping stones to the truth. Whatever they are, they should be examined, thought through. If you blindly follow something without thinking it through, then you're in trouble.

The endeavour should really be to turn belief into knowledge. That is a gradual process and comes about by putting your beliefs to the test of experience in order to find out whether they are genuine or not. This is the way to develop your own spiritual understanding.

It was in this process of looking at my own beliefs and prejudices that I first began to think about politics. By then I'd actually voted in several elections. It was high time I worked out where I stood and why.

Politics had never really been discussed in our family, but my parents were natural Conservatives and voted Conservative except on one occasion when they voted Labour for some reason. I don't remember why. There was no great political conviction in our house. There was no great religious conviction either. It seemed that there was no great conviction about anything, though it may be that my parents were simply too busy to discuss such things, as they worked jolly hard.

When I was away in the army my father was asked to stand for the local council as a Conservative member, and he said, 'Well, you can put me up if you like, but I'm not going to do any electioneering,' and he didn't, but he got elected all the same. It was a safe seat. But he wasn't a conviction politician and he was busy enough helping people as a doctor, so he served one term, which lasted three years, and that was that. He had dutifully attended the meetings he had had to attend, but he really didn't want to do it any more.

So I was of a naturally Conservative background, but I hadn't really thought about it too much. A lot of people vote a certain way because of the environment they're born into and grow up in, and I was like that. I'd just gone along with it. When I was growing up there'd been no indoctrination whatsoever, but there'd been no awareness either. So this was something that I started to look at.

By this time I had already got to know some politicians through the Street and had realized that certain people categorized others according to what party they belonged to, even thinking of them as party members rather than people. I thought it was ridiculous and my first reaction was not to like the political world very much. I knew that some politicians were wonderful, idealistic people, but a lot just seemed to be careerists. It also struck me that if you were a member of a party, you would distort the truth to defend your party. The minute a label is put on you, you have a tendency to defend that label, even against the truth. It's human nature, but I didn't like it and it seemed to me that that was what politics tended to be. I have always had great respect for anyone who has a sincere political view – I can happily sit with fascists, communists, Labour voters, Liberals, Conservatives, whatever, and hear their views, but if they start quacking dogma or there is a confrontation, then forget it, I don't want to know. I'm interested in discussions, not arguments.

The '60s were very interesting, politically. Everything was being broken down; it was a free-thinking era. At the time I was enjoying the freedom on a social level, but I wasn't aware of all the political developments. It's only with hindsight that I realize quite how radical it all was. During the early '70s, when I was thinking it all through, I began to understand the issues more. And although I fully sympathized and understood the necessity for the Labour movement and the unions, and I realized how wonderful some people in that movement could be, my leanings were towards greater individual freedom. I felt it was necessary for each person to take responsibility for their actions and to bear the consequences of those actions, rather than being told what to do. Labour is too hands on and interferes too much in our daily lives. So that led me to stay Conservative.

I have to say, though, politics was not high on my agenda then and never has been since. Thinking it through was really enough for me. I got to know Margaret Thatcher quite well in later years and went to Downing Street and Chequers, though. I am now quite friendly with George Osborne, who is my MP, and have met David Cameron quite a few times and like what he is doing.

As part of my search for the truth I also had a good look at astrology. Before that I would read my daily horoscope and, to my annoyance, would be affected by what I read. The reason for my annoyance was that I thought it had to be nonsense – how could all Taureans, from babies to old men, have the same experience on the same day? I put this to the doctor, expecting him to be dismissive of astrology, but he surprised me by saying, 'Go and study it and have some fun with it.'

He was always telling us to enjoy ourselves. Spiritual development should be a joy. It should never become a chore. If you're not enjoying yourself, if everything's hard work and you're lashing yourself onward, you might be sorting something out, but you're not really becoming a loving, joyous, happy person. There's great humour in being truly spiritual, which is something that people often forget. Dr Maugham knew about it, though, and, as I have mentioned, whenever he said goodbye, he would add, 'Enjoy yourself.' That was lovely, because we'd often had a very serious conversation – perhaps about battling with inner difficulties or facing up to outer problems – and it was a gentle reminder to lighten up.

I took a course with the Faculty of Astrological Studies, a highly reputable astrological college. It was a correspondence course, but I had a local tutor called Alice Back. I never met her, actually; it was all done through correspondence.

I learned to take the date, time and place of

birth and cast a chart showing the planets in their signs and houses and their aspects to each other, and then interpret it. That was initially a science, but as I improved I found that my intuition would sometimes play a part. After I'd drawn up a chart and drawn in the aspects, with different coloured inks and dotted lines or straight lines according to whether they were major or minor aspects, just by looking at it I'd get a feeling for the energy. Some charts looked gentle and harmonious and nicely balanced and some looked stark and a bit harsh. I suppose a really good astrologer would get to the point of being able to read a chart intuitively as well as intellectually.

When I first started there were no computers and it would take me a whole evening just to draw up a chart using logarithms. At school logarithms had been a nightmare and I hadn't seen the point of them, but now they were very, very useful. After a year of quite hard work, I passed the exam and received the certificate from the Faculty of Astrological Studies in 1976.

One of the first charts I did, of course, was my own. I checked out the dates of 23rd and 25th April and I'm inclined to think I was born on the 23rd, even though my birth certificate says the 25th. The little nursing home I was born in no longer existed, so there was no way of going back and checking the record.

Studying my own chart helped me to understand aspects of myself. I have a Grand Trine, which means a lot of good things will come to you fairly easily, and I've certainly been very lucky in many things, but I also have the sun square Saturn, which is just the opposite. That means you have to earn everything you get and work hard to keep it, otherwise it'll be taken from you. I could certainly see both of those aspects at work in my life. I could also see my Taurus sun in my love of good things and luxury, and tendency to put on weight, and my Gemini rising in my acting career. Your rising sign is the face you present to the world, the way other people see you. I also have Venus in the first house in Gemini, which would indicate a youthful appearance, and people have always commented that I have looked young for my age.

A lot of planets are in my twelfth house, which indicates that you'll come to things as you get older. Throughout my life I always seemed to be the last in things, to stay on a bit longer than everyone else, in almost everything I did – the Street is the perfect example. Anyway, it also means things will happen as I get older and that's nice in one sense, as it may mean I've got things to look forward to – though I'm probably there now!

Our personality, characteristics and traits are all there in our charts. I was able to establish this to my complete satisfaction. The reason behind this is that creation is swirling, moving and changing all the time, and when you're born, you reflect the pattern of the state of creation at that moment. You are of that time. So how do you look at that time? How do you understand what you are? The best way is to look at the largest moving things that we can see in creation, which are the planets. They are essentially symbols of the energy that is around at any given moment. From ancient times, people have observed that certain planets seem to indicate certain energies and therefore patterns of behaviour – Mars is energizing, Jupiter is beneficent, and so on. So astrology is really about reading the great movement of creation.

At one time sceptics often said that computers would prove once and for all that astrology was a fallacy. On the contrary, they have shown its validity. Large groups of people can now be studied for planetary influences and it has been found that certain planets feature strongly in certain professions. People in the armed forces will usually have Mars strongly positioned, for example, while for actors it is Jupiter – and all way beyond the laws of chance.

We do not have to be subject to these cosmic influences, as we have free will, but it is very helpful to know about them, and to know about ourselves, in order to work in harmony with the great plan. This is how astrology should be used. It's also worth bearing in mind that the strongest people are often those with the most difficult charts to overcome.

Also, there are periods when our personality is affected by the position of certain planets. There are difficult times and easy times, and these can be predicted. To be forewarned is to be forearmed.

I once had a phase when everything was hard going for me and nothing was working out, and when I looked at my chart I saw that Saturn was badly aspected to my sun. Saturn is the planet of limitation and restriction. However, I could also see when this would move away and things would get easier, so I knew I just had to take things steadily and wait for the better time.

I have also been able to appreciate how useful synastry – the comparison of the charts of two people in a relationship – can be. This was brought home to me when I was asked to do the chart of the girlfriend of someone I knew. I had not met the girl, as she lived in Holland, and knew nothing about her. She happened to have a very striking chart, so it was possible to give a very clear description of her personality and characteristics. My friend couldn't believe how accurate this was, and said that I was very clever. 'No,' I said. 'It's not that I'm clever, but that astrology is true.'

Quite a few colleagues on *Coronation Street* also asked me to cast their charts and were impressed by their accuracy.

Astrology should be used as a tool on our journey of understanding. What it does is inform us. Obviously, in any situation, the more information you have, the better your judgement will be. So you should use it to inform yourself, but not let it dictate to you, as some people do. You're not governed by it. But it does help you to understand yourself and the forces around your particular situation.

'The personality evolves in time.
The soul evolves in eternity.'

Astrology also helps us to see our relationship with the universe. It is impossible to look at the order in the cyclic movement of the planets and to recognize its similarity with the movement within an atom without realizing the presence of an infinite intelligence.

And, fortunately, it is also possible to have a little fun with it. So I did manage to enjoy myself.

Having proven to myself there was a validity in it, however, after a while I stopped using it. I don't really know why. It's strange to know that something has validity but not use it. I think I realized that what I really needed at that stage was to work on myself. I knew that at the end of the day astrology didn't make the decisions. Astrology can assist you, but it won't do anything for you. That's up to you. So I left it for a while and carried on with my development in other ways.

One of these was to become a director of a company which publishes the *Lancashire Magazine*, in which I write the monthly astrology column. But more of that later. In the meantime, big changes were in store.

CHAPTER 11

Settling Down

*'Peace does not come from without
but from within.'*

As I was changing, so were many other things in my life. Unfortunately, my wayward behaviour had put my marriage under too much strain and it was breaking down. My first wife Anna and I were eventually divorced in 1974. We hadn't had rows, we had simply become estranged, and I knew that it was all my fault. We had drifted apart and I wasn't proud of that because I was the offender. I remember one occasion when Anna came up north and found under the pillow a handkerchief left there by a girl who had visited the previous night. I tried to explain it away by saying it had been lent to me by an actress who was playing my wife at the time in the Street, but I was fooling no one.

Personal failures like this are also lessons.

What you have to do is to take the positive view of such a situation, if you can, and move forward. No good will come of looking back in regret. It is worth checking over any errors you've made to make sure you don't repeat them, but then you have to look forward and go forward.

'Failures are a means of learning the lessons of how to succeed.'

I think if you have failed in one marriage and you have the chance to make a success of another, you've been given a great opportunity to learn. If you can make a success of the second marriage, it may be that you can do in one lifetime something that might have taken two incarnations. I don't know. But you've definitely been given a second chance and you should make darn sure that you don't make the mistakes you made the first time.

I was lucky enough to be given such a chance.

It came about because Dick Everett, the producer of *Coronation Street*, asked me to attend a fund-raising evening for charity. He and his wife were members of an amateur dramatics society, the Green Room, in

Wilmslow, and they were hosting an event based on the television programme *Going for a Song*, where antiques were brought on and you had to try and guess what they were. He asked if I would go along and take part. I was a bit busy, but I made the fatal mistake of saying, 'If you can't get anybody else, come back.' Well, of course he couldn't get anybody else and he came back and I did it. A very glamorous model called Sara Mottram brought on the antiques. Her parents were also involved with the Green Room, but I later found out that she hadn't been very keen on being there either.

Halfway through, there was an interval and I went out to ask where the loo was. Sara told me, and as she did so, she brushed some fluff off my jacket. That was all, but as I was walking away it suddenly came to her that she was going to marry me. Somehow she just knew it. Now I say, 'Well, you never warned me, did you?' I have since learned that her intuition is very powerful. In particular her feelings about people on first meeting are very rarely wrong.

That night we got to know each other at the party afterwards, and it went on from there. At the time I had come to the end of one marriage and had no thoughts of remarrying at all. Nevertheless we did get wed five years later, in 1977. It was a very quiet registry office ceremony as neither of us wanted any fuss. I simply took the day off from *Coronation Street* and kept the arrangements very quiet. It has proved to be a wonderful marriage and Sara and I are one of showbusiness's most enduring couples.

> *'Where hangs the key to the mysteries of heaven? It hangs in the heart.'*

There are things that you suddenly feel are right. You don't really know why, but you are completely comfortable with them. This was how it felt with Sara. It might be an example of an agreement made before incarnation. I don't know. Perhaps, without really knowing it, I had developed enough to be ready for a different kind of relationship. Whatever the case, I was now totally satisfied with married life and didn't feel the need to look elsewhere. All my restlessness had vanished and I was more than happy to settle down. It was such a relief.

Sara had been involved with acting herself, so she knew how everything worked, and she certainly wasn't awestruck by the fact that I was on national television. She simply took it all in her stride. I was a little miffed, though, to learn that when *Coronation Street* had started she had fancied my brother, Alan Rothwell, not me!

I was still with *Coronation Street*, of course, though there were times when I was about 40 when I wondered whether I should be getting out. I hadn't ever made a conscious decision to stay with it – it had just been a year at a time. There had been a couple of occasions when we had been on three-year contracts, but generally the contract was for one year, and that's generally what it is now. You expect to be offered a new contract, but you might not be. When you hear that *Coronation Street* actors are 'sacked', technically they're not. It's just that their contracts haven't been renewed. Anyway, I thought things through and stayed with it – a year at a time. I like to think I am no different from anyone else in the cast but occasionally I get a little reminder that in some respects perhaps I am: at the height of an emotional scene with Deirdre quite recently, I couldn't think of a key word and let out an expletive. 'Blimey,' said the sound guy, 'that was like hearing your grandmother swear!'

Life is always moving on, but I've always

been one who likes to hang on to things. I'd like a good strong car that would last forever. I'd like a good strong house. But nothing is permanent. I hadn't fully realized this then. I was always looking for permanence. So it is not surprising that I am in the most permanent form of employment a very uncertain profession has to offer.

I had the good strong house too, or rather bungalow. After living for six or seven years in the cottage at Rawtenstall I had bought two cottages nearby, together with nearly an acre of land. I had renovated one, sold the other and built a bungalow on the land. It had three-fifths of an acre of garden which I planted with apple trees. Sara and I lived there for several years and were very happy there.

By this time Dr Maugham had died, but he had left me a wonderful spiritual legacy. When he died, I carried on – as he said, you should follow your interests.

One thing Dr Maugham taught us, which remained with me, was the importance of thought. We tend to think that a thought is just a thought, but it is an *energy*. It goes out, has an effect and then returns, loaded up with whatever its content was. So you get back what you give out. All your good thoughts will return with good energy and all your bad thoughts will return to harm you. So it is better to send out good thoughts, if only for self-preservation! Most of our thoughts are muddled, chaotic and half-baked, so it's no wonder that we're living in a messy jumble of semi-darkness instead of a beautiful, clear, loving world.

As I continued my development I became more aware of the power of thought. Nowadays, if I am ever with a large group of noisy people and am beginning to think unkind thoughts about them, I will remind myself that we are all eternal beings on a journey and will bring to mind a wonderful thought: 'Dear everyone, I love you all.' Immediately I will feel relaxed. The people and the noise may be the same, but by changing my thoughts, I have changed my response.

We can do this all the time. We can't always change what happens to us, but we can change how we react. This fundamental truth can work miracles. Try it. If someone is being really horrible to you, first forgive them and then send them loving thoughts. You will be astounded how often the situation changes completely.

As I continued to explore spiritually,

243

something wonderful happened to me – my fears of death and infinity started to diminish. Once my mind was opened up and I realized that although there was more to life than I could see and hear and feel and touch, that was fine, the fear began to subside. Infinity seemed far less threatening. And when I was taught that we were eternal beings and were all infinitely loved, 'infinite' became a good word, an exciting word. Infinity was a wonderful thing.

'God is the spirit of infinite love.'

Realizing that there was life after death also helped me tremendously. Once you realize that, the fear of death goes totally. Now I'm really looking forward to death, though I don't like the idea of actually dying. But even that is alleviated by the fact that you know that it is a great release and that you're going home.

I once saw how wonderful death could be. I knew an army officer in London and met his mother a couple of times. She was a nice old dear. One day when I rang my friend and asked how she was, he said, 'Oh, I'm afraid she's in hospital. She's dying.' I went to see her and she was lying back with her eyes closed. I just sat down beside her and suddenly she opened her eyes and looked at me and said, 'Hello.' That was all, but it was the most beautiful look. It said, 'You don't feel sorry for me, do you?' And she herself was radiant. She died that evening.

Later on I saw the same thing with my father. The night he died, my mother and sister and I were sitting with him and my sister was holding one of his hands and I was holding the other. Without a word, he looked from one of us to the other and his eyes looked big and childlike and really quite beautiful. And he died not long after that.

As my fears were subsiding, I was continuing to grow in awareness. I realized that in order to learn the great truths, the lower self has to be tamed and overcome. This is symbolized by St George and the dragon, the dragon representing the passions of the lower self. The lower self will argue, fight, kill and do all sorts of other awful things, but the spiritual self just wants to love everybody. If we could all just allow our spiritual selves to shine through, all the problems of the world would be solved. We wouldn't even need the Earth any more as a school.

'Through God's wisdom we are taught and guided, but never punished.'

In the meantime, though, we all have to tame the lower self. It is a slow process and cannot be rushed, but through self-improvement on the one hand and daily meditation on the other we slowly move onwards and upwards. There is reading and learning to be done and gentle self-discipline. Gentle self-discipline is better than harsh measures, as the lower self is overcome by releasing the peace and love in the heart region and this is a process of letting go and cannot be forced.

Essentially, all we have to do is let love shine out through every aspect of our being and eventually radiate out to others through love and service. This is easily said, of course, but the lower self will hang on and fight for its own survival. At the beginning I saw this as a battle and it caused me a lot of inner turmoil. I felt angry and frustrated. Then I learned the big lesson, that love conquers all. If we love the lower self, it ceases to dominate. So don't despise the lower self, just love it and rise above it.

Becoming aware is the first step. If you just observe your behaviour, as Dr Maugham taught us, you may notice that your language is a little coarser than it should be or that you enjoy criticizing people too much. Don't be discouraged – the fact that you have noticed these traits is the first sign of your rising awareness. The next step is to modify these things whenever you can, without despairing when they do happen. Gradually they will be eliminated and you will become aware of other negative traits to work on. You are on your way.

Once you become more aware, you will find that your higher self is able to come through more clearly and help you in all aspects of your life. In the beginning it can only contact you through inspiration, intuition and dreams. For this reason, intuition is always to be relied upon more than reason. How many times, against all the odds, has a woman's intuition proved to be right? Look at my experience with Sara when she said she knew we were going to be married. Similarly, when you have a bright idea that affects the direction of your life, where did that come from? Then there are those dreams that seem more real than the others – like the one I had in which Dr Maugham appeared so dramatically – and bring with them a feeling that stays with you all day. All these are ways in which your higher self is making contact.

> *'All that is necessary to contact the divine is the thought, "God hold me, God keep me."'*

We also have spiritual guides and helpers trying to impress on our minds the thoughts that will lead us in the right direction. As I understand it, we all have a major spiritual guide. Some people call it a guardian angel. Whatever term you choose, it is a being who is really looking out for us. We usually also have spirit friends helping us, people we knew in other incarnations. They have chosen to do this work. Like the higher self, they may communicate with us through dreams, sudden ideas, 'chance' meetings or something we read in a book. All the time we're being influenced and aided by loving spiritual guides.

Over time I have come to recognize the influence of my guide in my life more and more, and at times I can even feel its presence. It's a wonderful warm glow. I can't identify the particular individual, but then I don't need to. It's definitely a loving presence and that's all I need to know. Of course I'd love to be able to say, 'It's so-and-so. Oh hello, how are you?' I have met mediums who know their guides personally and that's a really nice relationship to have. But just to know that your guide is there is a lovely feeling. Everyone, without exception, has one and I am grateful that I have been made so acutely aware of that.

It has been fairly late in life that I have become aware of this, but looking back I can see there were many moments when I had feelings or ideas that definitely came from my guide. As we develop spiritually this process becomes clearer and more frequent, and if we consciously choose to be receptive, it can become an open contact. Ultimately, when we have awakened completely, there is direct communication. This is the true meaning of being born again. The first birth is natural; the second is spiritual.

This is a path that we are all treading, consciously or unconsciously. Those who are not aware are nudged and directed by their life's experiences. Those who become aware can learn in a more conscious and controlled way. Ultimately, the whole purpose of life is to bring us to the realization of our oneness with infinite love, to unfold ourselves spiritually.

'Every soul has to find reality at some time.

The task can be delayed, but it cannot be averted forever.'

For now, if you wish to experience the presence of your guardian angel, if you open yourself to it and ask for it, it will happen. It might not happen in the way that you think it will, but it will happen all the same. Your angel will make itself known.

While I was doing this inner work, on an outer level life was also opening out. Sara was a good actress and I wanted to branch out a little and produce some plays, so we set up a production company together, William Roache Productions. Vin Sumner, the manager of the Charter Theatre at the Guildhall in Preston, was very encouraging and we produced four plays there. The first was Noël Coward's *Blithe Spirit*. I was the lead and Sara played my wife. Everything went well, though on the first night I was so nervous that my hand shook violently as I was handing over some drinks on stage. It wasn't until we were rehearsing the second play, André Roussin's *The Little Hut*, a comedy about three people who are shipwrecked on a desert island, that the dreaded giggles struck. At one point Brian Mosley, who played Alf

Roberts in *Coronation Street*, the director Diana Harker and I were all absolutely helpless with laughter.

Obviously this sort of thing is a real disadvantage to an actor. I'm afraid I have always found it very difficult to control and at one time I was afraid I'd have to give up acting altogether because of it. Now I have developed a technique of turning away and thinking of something serious, but it's not always easy. On *Coronation Street* Eileen Derbyshire, who plays Emily Bishop, is also prone to fits of giggles, and if we have a tense or dramatic scene together and something sets us off, it can be very tricky to manage. Still, apparently Olivier was a giggler too, so it can happen to the best of actors.

The Little Hut turned out well in the end, but we used six tons of sand to get an authentic desert island effect and they were still trying to get rid of it years later.

After that we did another couple of shows at Preston, *Flip Side*, a farce by Margaret Williams and Hugh Steadman Williams, and Alan Ayckbourn's *Time and Time Again*. We broke even with all of them, and for a new company without a subsidy and in a theatre without a regular audience, I thought that was pretty good. All the while I was on stage in the evenings I was still filming *Coronation Street* by day, though, and it was an exhausting schedule. It would have been impossible to keep up for long.

Next we produced two Sunday-night chat shows introduced by Gordon Burns. The first had Cliff Richard – whom I know well – as a guest and the second was the wonderful Frankie Vaughan. Cliff revealed that he was a great fan of *Coronation Street* and that after Minnie Caldwell called him 'that chubby Cliff Richard' in 1964, he adopted a sensible diet to which he has adhered ever since.

Producing shows was an education for me. For the first time I really became aware of all the responsibilities and pressures faced by management. I also grew to hate auditioning actors – particularly as I wanted to give everyone the part! As time went on I learned that actors who read well at audition might not do so well on stage and it's always best to see them work if you can.

The production company had been a fascinating experience, but we simply didn't have the time to devote to it, and it was almost with relief that I went back to 'just' playing Ken on *Coronation Street*.

In 1981 Sara gave birth to our first daughter, Verity, and we needed more room, so we moved to Sykeside House, a Victorian former mill owner's house nearby. This was a beautiful three-storey mansion of honey-coloured stone with a lovely old garden and two-and-a-half acres of land. There was a weeping ash in the front drive which reminded me of the one at Rutland House and I always felt very at home there.

I still had the tendency to try to do things for myself, even if I didn't have the required expertise, and when we moved I decided to do the conveyancing myself. If both houses had been registered and there hadn't been any boundary problems this would have been straightforward; unfortunately, everything was far more complicated than I had envisaged. Then, as if all this wasn't enough, the man buying my bungalow died. At that, I gave up and brought in a solicitor. Sometimes you have to recognize when you have taken on too much. It was a useful lesson.

All the while, fame was opening doors. I had been invited to join the Variety Club Golf Society and really enjoyed taking part in their tournaments. A celebrity and a professional would play with two amateurs, who paid to do so, which was how they raised money for charity. Lots of celebrities also had their own golf tournaments and I was delighted to become part of the circuit. Since then I've also played in pro-celebrity tournaments on television. I found that golf can be like meditation in that you have to harmonize your body, mind and emotions. In fact I found that meditating actually improved my golf!

Thinking about fame, it seems to me that there are three stages of it. The first is when it's new. That's all very nice. You enjoy all the attention. But then suddenly you go into the next phase and realize that once you're known, you can't become unknown. For the first time you learn how restrictive it can be. You can't go incognito anywhere and if you're doing anything wrong, the press are going to be on it in a minute. This can get quite frightening and claustrophobic, because you feel you can't get away from it. Some people suffer quite badly. For those who have fame very briefly or who court it and then suddenly don't want it, it can be a particularly difficult thing.

Once you've had the time to adjust, however, you simply learn to live with it. That's the phase that I'm in now. I know I'm no better or no worse than anybody else just because I'm famous. I have a job that exposes me to the public and that's it. There are advantages and there are disadvantages, but I would say the advantages outweigh the disadvantages.

Apart from the golf, one of the advantages is the influence you can have. Well, actually I'm not sure whether I have had any influence on anybody, but you do get asked to give your views on a wide range of subjects – often ones you know nothing about.

In the early '80s we decided to move from Sykeside House, as there were no schools nearby, and move to Wilmslow, Sara's birthplace. She was keen to move back there. Her parents were still living there and it was delightful to be so close to them. In April 1983 our second daughter, Edwina, was born. I was working at Granada and although it was only a 20-minute journey from the studios to the Davy Hume Hospital where Sara was giving birth, the birth was so quick that I almost didn't make it. It was, I remember, a lovely sunny day, so suitable for the arrival of such a beautiful child whom we affectionately nicknamed Teddy. There was, of course, no inkling of the sad, sad event which was to occur the following year.

It was coming up to June and the 1983 General Election, and I was beginning to be concerned about the outcome. I felt that

Mrs Thatcher, as she then was, was a strong and sincere leader who was taking the country forward. I know many people will disagree with this, but it was my honest view. So I decided to do what I could to help her re-election.

In general, actors tend to keep their political opinions quiet for fear of alienating people. Whatever your political orientation, you are bound to upset potentially quite a broad section of the population. But I felt that now was the time to make my feelings known. Also, I didn't really like the fact that because Ken Barlow was a committed socialist, a lot of people automatically assumed that I was too. I wanted to stand up for my own beliefs.

When I ran into the local Conservative MP, Neil Hamilton, and his wife Christine at a craft exhibition at Wilmslow library, I said, 'If I can be of any help with the election, will you let me know?'

'But,' he said, 'I thought you were—'

'No,' I replied simply, 'I'm not.'

'Not everything is as it seems.'

After that I spent a very busy few weeks making appearances with Neil and other local

Conservative MPs. I found this was very different from opening fêtes and so on as a celebrity. When you make those kind of appearances you get the happy impression that everyone loves you. But now I had people being aggressive and shouting things like 'I'm not going to watch your show any more!' It could be unnerving. But on the whole more people were pleasant than hostile.

When Margaret Thatcher held a rally at Chester, I was invited along to meet her. I found her attentive and interested in what we had to say. She also seemed quite vulnerable in a way, not at all like her harsh image. She actually asked Sara and me what she could do to overcome that – the harsh image – and I told her, 'Well, I just wish everyone could meet you.'

Above all, what I liked about Margaret Thatcher was that she was a conviction politician. Rightly or wrongly, she believed certain things were right for the country and she was determined to see them through. I think convictions are terribly important.

As my views became more widely known, I was invited to give after-dinner speeches to Conservative groups all round the country and I met many other members of parliament. I was also fortunate to have the pleasure of visiting Mrs Thatcher twice at Downing Street. The first time was just after the Falklands War and she took me through to the Cabinet Room. I thought she wouldn't talk about the war, but she chatted very openly about getting the *Queen Mary* commissioned for it and how she felt about it. I found her very sensitive. I know she could seem alarming and quite strident, but that was because she was a person of great conviction. She only began to fail when she started listening to others. Interestingly, though, there usually comes a time when your own convictions may not be in everyone's best interests; then it is time to go. What I don't like about politics today is that people seem to have so few convictions. They'll do anything to make themselves look good and to appease public opinion. They'll go for immediate results rather than do unpopular things, but they'll say they're doing it for the long term if it all goes wrong. I think they're all focusing on face-saving rather than doing what they feel to be right. Having said that, I must thank Cherie Blair for producing a wonderful chocolate cake on my last visit to Downing Street, which happened (and goodness knows how she knew) to coincide with my birthday.

I don't think being a politician is an easy job – I wouldn't want to be one for anything – and there are certainly some good honest people involved in politics who feel it is their way of contributing to society. However, so much of the media coverage focuses on the personal weaknesses of ministers or the faults of a particular policy, and that leads to political life becoming a big game of survival rather than a form of responsible leadership. It's a hard game.

Life itself can be very hard, as I was about to find out.

CHAPTER 12

Love and Loss

*'If your life on Earth had no struggle
you could count the experience
a complete loss.'*

The biggest test that I had, and the most tragic moment of my life, also gave me a beautiful spiritual experience. On 16 November 1984 my daughter Edwina died at the age of 18 months.

For about a week she had had a bad cold and we had called in the doctor, who had prescribed antibiotics and linctus. She was soon cool and comfortable and we thought she was on the mend. That night Sara's parents, Sid and Kay, came round to babysit so that she and I could go out for a Chinese meal.

On returning from dinner Sara went up to see Edwina and found her sleeping peacefully. We talked to Sid and Kay for about half an hour, then they left for home.

As soon as they had gone Sara went up to see Edwina once again and found her lying motionless at the top of her cot. She was dead. We called the ambulance and I tried the kiss of life, to no avail. When the medical staff arrived they did all they could, but it was too late. It was not a cot death; it was a form of acute bronchitis.

Our children are not supposed to die before us. We are supposed to protect and look after them. So on top of the great grief at losing a child, there is the feeling of guilt because, as parents, it is something that we should not allow to happen. Though rationally Sara and I knew we had done all we could for our daughter, still we couldn't help feeling that we had let her down in some way. We could not talk without bursting into tears; we could not eat. For three days we lived on hot chocolate. We couldn't face going out of the house. We tried not to cry in front of Verity, who was three at the time, and to explain to her what had happened to her sister. But it was so difficult. We were utterly devastated. We went to bed the night before the funeral not knowing how we were going to get through the ceremony.

When I woke in the morning it was light. I lay there for a while preparing myself for the awful day ahead and then the most extraordinary thing happened. I suddenly saw the most beautiful golden light and in the middle of it was Edwina's face. She was looking down, smiling at me as if to say, 'Don't worry. All is well and I am happy.' All at once I had the most wonderful feeling of peace and I knew I could go forward.

From that moment on I gained strength. I told Sara, and although she hadn't seen Edwina, she said that she too felt a lot stronger. So although only I saw it, the experience was sent for both of us. It helped us enormously to get through the funeral and I carried Edwina's coffin with a confidence I could never have mustered without it.

For four or five days after the funeral I still felt the guilt and grief as a physical pain, but I was aware that to some extent that was conditioning. At that time I already had enough spiritual understanding to realize that this would have been pre-planned and that we would all have chosen to experience it for a particular reason. After several days of intense grieving – which is totally understandable as the parent of a child – the true understanding came in and I realized that Edwina would have decided to incarnate just for a short while. It was a great lesson to learn and it wasn't long before we were able to think about how much we had enjoyed the short time she had been with us rather than just feel sad about the fact that she had gone.

I also knew that she would be in a very loving place and would be very well cared for and that we would meet again.

In fact, as I mentioned in the Preface, several years later I did hear from Edwina again. In the early '90s I received a letter from a remarkable woman, Peggy Kennard, who had seen me on the *Heaven & Earth* show one Sunday morning and realized that I had some understanding of spiritual matters. Peggy was an advanced soul with great wisdom and the ability to contact spirit. We stayed in touch for many years. She would send me spiritual books and excerpts that were always amazingly helpful and appropriate to my needs. She would also send me messages she had received from spirit. These were always accurate and very useful.

One day she wrote to say she hoped that I would not mind but she had received a message from Edwina. *Mind?* It was the most wonderful news imaginable. The message was long and detailed. Edwina started with an accurate explanation of who she was and went on to say that she had contacted Peggy because she was a friend of mine and that she 'shone out like a beacon' and was easy to get in touch with. She described her as 'our finely tuned instrument'.

Edwina went on to say that she was very happy and was now working with young children who had arrived in the spiritual realms and, not knowing anything was different, were crying for their mothers. I realized that my daughter was a very beautifully evolved spiritual being doing great work. It was a beautiful feeling to have this communication from her.

Peggy's messages were always loving,

strong and informative. They ceased after a few years when Peggy herself went to the spiritual realms. She can now talk to Edwina face to face.

As I understand it, death occurs when the vibration of the body reaches a certain point and its destiny is fulfilled. So, unless you decide to commit suicide, you never go until your time is right. Then the body releases the spirit. That is a great liberation. We are all spiritual beings held temporarily in a material body and when we return to the spiritual realms we are free to be our true selves, our spiritual selves, with all the attributes, all the experiences, wisdom and worth that we have developed through various incarnations.

If we've had a traumatic death or a painful death, first of all we have a sleeping period, a resting period. That's just to give us the chance to recover. When we wake, we will always find loved ones around us, ready to welcome us and help us, and we will be in the most beautiful place. People often say, 'Oh, that's wishful thinking, it's just a philosophy of convenience,' but it isn't.

This first level of the spirit realms, where we wake, is the astral. It's the nearest level to

Earth. As I mentioned earlier, every night while we are sleeping we visit it and actively participate in the life there, but we are unable to retain the memory on returning to our bodies. This is why sleep is so essential, because while the causal body is out on the astral, the physical body is repairing all the damage that has been done during the day.

At some point soon after we have passed over we will review the life we have just lived. We will look at it and see what we've done, assess the good and the bad. We aren't judged by others; we are our own judge. But we have guides and helpers who will assist us.

Eventually we will leave the astral and go to the level of our worth. There are realms ranging from the dark and unpleasant to the bright and heavenly, and most of us are destined for one somewhere in the middle. This will be a much brighter and freer version of life as we know it now, only there will be no physical needs, illnesses or death, as we are immortal. There will just be the eternal task of improving our state of being, searching for the truth and raising our consciousness.

People would lead far better lives if they knew that in the spiritual realms they went to the level of their worth. There is a mansion waiting for them, but what is its condition, what is the state of the neighbourhood and who are their neighbours? That will depend on how they have lived their lives. But there is no such thing as eternal damnation; anyone, however bad, will get help if they ask for it.

'God never gives in. The god within us all waits with divine patience for the lesson to be learned.'

We will also be able to meet up with all our loved ones again, even our pets. People often say, 'How, if you've had previous lives and previous husbands or wives, can you all exist happily together?' But if there is genuine love between people, they will be together. And it's nothing to do with whether you're married or not married, it's all to do with love. If there's love between two people, they will be together. And there'll be no possessive jealousy as there is here. In the spiritual realms it is understood that we all really love everybody. As eternal beings we love all other eternal beings. We have a different perspective there.

It may be of course that the level you are

living on is different from that of someone you love, because we all go to the level of our worth. But there's nothing to stop you from meeting up and being together whenever you wish. Love is a great connector.

Animals also have their own domain, but if you love an animal, it will come to you and stay with you for a certain length of time. At some point, though, you have to let animals go, because it is alien to their line of development to remain with you forever. But initially, the animals that you've loved will be with you.

People often tend to think that when they go to their true home in the spiritual realm they'll suddenly know all the great truths. Unfortunately this is not the case. We still have to undergo a learning process. But there are many opportunities to do this at all levels. There are universities, music schools, art schools, libraries – anything you want. And there are always people willing to help you. Great work can be done in the spiritual realms. All great ideas and inventions are created there and then passed down to the Earth plane through flashes of inspiration.

You can make real progress in the spiritual realms, but eventually there will come a time when you will see that you need to discharge some negative energy and the only way to do that is to incarnate again on Earth. That will be worked out in advance by you yourself with help from higher beings. This is a hard school and we usually don't want to come back here. Our loved ones in the spiritual realms will miss us too. There's often great sorrow as somebody departs to incarnate, but an incarnation is nevertheless a great opportunity.

As I understand it, you incarnate into a family and an area that is right for you; a lot of other souls, of similar age in terms of soul development, may come in at the same time. Whenever anyone has a real effect on you during your earthly life, there will be a reason for it. You may have agreed together to perform certain roles in advance in order to give each other the chance to experience a particular situation and to learn from it.

As well as the Earth, there are other worlds into which we can incarnate. They may not be within our solar system. The other planets in our solar system are not currently inhabited by beings of a physical nature (well, not of our vibrational level) but probably were in the past. But there are other planets, around other suns, that offer other types of material existence, either more refined or less refined than ours. Even the most hard-nosed scientist looking out into the cosmos will say that according to the law of probability there have to be other planets out there in other solar systems with life approximately like ours.

I read once in a spiritual book – and I can only go by the fact that what I was reading seemed to be genuine in every other respect – that the Earth is not the densest of the material worlds; there is one other that is denser, lower in vibration. And there are others to suit every need. Then the time comes when you do not need to incarnate and continue to evolve only in the spiritual realms.

Once we understand reincarnation we also understand that we are responsible for ourselves and our actions and that it is in our own interest to improve ourselves.

Once we have learned all the lessons that can possibly be learned from material existence, then we don't need to incarnate any more. To reach that point, though, you've got to be what we would call absolutely saintly, totally spiritual and selfless and totally loving and compassionate, so most of us have a long way to go!

Great teachers who have reached that

point actually often choose to come back because they love humanity and want to help. There are masters here on Earth right now, highly evolved beings, but you would pass them by on the street. They usually keep a low profile and do their work quietly and unobtrusively with those who are ready to work with them.

Knowing all this, of course you can still experience great grief when someone dies. Sara and I suffered terribly at first. With some couples, a loss splits them totally, because they grieve in different ways, but Sara and I talked our way through it and helped each other through it. So there was a learning process, though not a conscious one – often learning is not conscious, something deeper is there – and then we grew to accept that it was wonderful to have had Edwina for the 18 months that we did.

It's understandable to grieve when someone leaves you and it can be particularly hard to deal with if they have had a painful death. But often a painful death is in itself the discharging of great negative energy and that soul will grow and benefit from it. It's hard for us to see that, of course. But every death that you experience in your life is part of your destiny and there is something to learn from every one.

When someone dies, there's no need to worry about them. They've gone home, they've finished their toil, their time at school. They're been released – early maybe, because they've done a good job. It's understandable to miss someone you love and feel sad that they aren't around, although they are, in a sense. You are upset by the loss of contact. But that's not forever either. Love is the great connector and if someone was close to you they are only a thought away. So if you are grieving for someone, just send them love and say, 'Well done. I miss you, of course, but we'll meet again.'

This is where the Church, because it doesn't truly understand life after death, is unable to help people in times of bereavement. But when you understand that the person who has died is fine and happy and has gone home and that you will be with them again, that's a great comfort. In the meantime they will be missing you too, but they know they can send love to you and every loving thought is instantly received. If you wish, you can send them the thought, *I love you and will continue to love you and I hope all is well*, and they will receive it. It's good to know that.

Essentially, the best way to work through bereavement is to understand that our permanent home before and after reincarnation is the spiritual realms, which are beautiful, vital, living, bright places. So anyone who has died has gone home. They've been through their illnesses, they've been through their turmoil and now they are wonderfully happy. So you don't need to grieve for them. You will miss them, but you can still send them thoughts and you know you'll meet again. I think once you have that understanding it helps you to get over a loss quite quickly. It's only temporary, after all.

One friend of mine who really couldn't understand my certainty about life after death – or my support for the Conservative Party! – was Selwyn Hughes. We stayed in touch after our time in Jamaica and remained friends until his death just last year. After the army our lives took very different directions. Selwyn was a very intellectual guy and, as he had hoped, he eventually went to Oxford University. After that he became a professor of English and poetry at Harlech University before emigrating to Australia. His poetry was widely respected.

We were quite dissimilar in many ways and this resulted in some great conversations. We couldn't agree on anything to do with the afterlife at all. Through this I came to realize that a strong intellect can be a real problem in terms of gaining a spiritual understanding.

'Those who have knowledge do not always have wisdom.'

Wealth can be the same. It took me a long time to understand that while there is nothing wrong with wealth per se, a wealthy person can have great problems making spiritual progress. Such a person is so comfortable with his or her material life they lack the motivation to look elsewhere. It is the eye-of-a-needle syndrome. The wealthy have to spend a disproportionate amount of time looking after their wealth and that is inevitably at the expense of their spiritual health. Wealthy people have a great gift. They have acquired the ability to make money and this can give employment to many and expand businesses. There are two things a wealthy person needs to be wary of; one is that no one is exploited or harmed, and the other is that they find sufficient time for their spiritual health.

Selwyn wasn't particularly wealthy, but he had such a strong mind he could rationalize everything away. 'No, you're talking rubbish,' he'd say whenever I mentioned anything to do with life after death. 'Where's the proof?'

There will never be any general proof of life after death, but if any individual asks for proof it will be given to them. If you, reading this now, want proof of life after death, it can be yours. If you are sincere in this, here is what you have to do.

Think clearly to yourself, *I would like to understand more and I would like proof that there is life after death.* Think this as often as you can, but especially last thing at night before going to sleep. Your own spiritual self, your guardian angel and other helpers who are around you are receiving this thought.

Then open yourself up and wait. Don't anticipate or expect anything. Just wait. Sooner or later something will happen to prove the existence of life after death to you. There is no time limit. It will happen quicker for some than for others. It may even be that you have tired of making the request, stopped and forgotten about it. But the proof will still come because you have put out the call. Do not be impatient, be sincere and the proof *will* be yours. When it comes, you will recognize it and oh, what joy! You will know you are a spiritual being and in contact with others. You are on your way! This proof will not come in a way that you can pass on to others, but you will see it for what it is.

Unfortunately Selwyn didn't want to know any of this. It was particularly sad because he'd lost a son at around 10 years old. They had been going to a football match together and his son had stepped off the pavement and been hit by a lorry. Selwyn always felt guilty because he hadn't been able to protect him. I tried to tell him that his son was fine, but he wouldn't have it. It actually got to the point where he said, 'If you start talking like that, you know we won't go on.' And yet we were great friends.

The thing is, you should never be judgemental and condemn anyone for what they do or what they believe. We're all at different stages of the process. Selwyn and I certainly had very different ideas. He would say to me, 'I can't understand why we're friends. I'm a Marxist and you're a Conservative and know Margaret Thatcher!'

There's no such thing as coincidence, of

course, and the fact that Selwyn and I were close friends for so many years meant that we each had a lot to learn from the other. He had the mind that I would have liked to have and I had a spiritual understanding that maybe now he will have because he's gone to the spiritual realms. I expect he'll be saying, 'Okay, Bill, you were right about that. Sorry about that.' Unfortunately he could still be saying, 'I'm a Marxist!' I haven't heard anything from him. It's early days and he may still be sleeping. The rest period usually goes on for quite a while.

I do believe that you choose the people who come in and join you in your life, some as enemies, some as friends. To a large extent it is planned, but it's up to you how you handle it. You have free will, though only up to a point. You can't change the major events that happen to you but you can very much change how you respond to those events. And at the end of the day the whole point is to learn to love and serve.

So everything has a reason, even the most awful thing. And everybody is struggling for spiritual unfoldment, whether they know it or not.

CHAPTER 13

On and Off the Street

'Adverse experiences are priceless gifts that hold a promise of better things to come.'

When Edwina died, all my colleagues were terrifically sympathetic and supportive, and even the press managed to show a modicum of decency. Pretty early on a reporter knocked on our door and told us that a pack of reporters was at the gate. He asked us what we wanted them to do. 'Would you please leave us alone?' I said, and they did.

We also received a huge amount of support from total strangers. Letters arrived from all over the country and Sara and I were touched by the concern and the thoughtfulness that people had shown. Knowing that there were so many good, caring people out there gave us both strength.

Many of the letters were from people who had suffered a similar loss and I felt I was able to share something with them. I wrote back to as many of them as I could and I hope I was able to offer them some comfort.

Of course, people knew what was happening to me because by then in a sense *Coronation Street* had become part of the national consciousness. Nobody had anticipated that. It hadn't been expected to last for very long, really. When it started, it did have a special quality, though. It is still highly respected but after 15–20 years similar shows started up and gradually we got surrounded and the term 'soap' came in and people started calling us 'Corrie'. It hurt to be called 'just a soap'.

I'm not complaining, though. Working on *Coronation Street* is very rewarding. You get scenes in it that are as good as you're going to get anywhere. One of the directors once said to me, 'You know, these particular scenes here are as good as you'd find in an "A" feature film or a West End play.' I know that after some of the bust-up scenes with Deirdre I would find myself in floods of tears, which is a testimony to the high quality of the writing. Every so often you're hitting really good stuff. There's job satisfaction there, certainly. And it's nice to know it's popular. We still top the ratings, there still is something special about the show and we've been going for longer than any other serial anywhere, I think, which says something. When you think that children who started watching it at their mother's knee have now not only got children but in some cases also grandchildren growing up watching it, you know that you're really reaching people.

One compliment I received for my work gave me particular pleasure. One day back in the '70s I was on the phone in the studio corridor and as I put the receiver down, a voice behind me said, 'I would just like to say how much I enjoy your performance in *Coronation Street*.'

I turned round to find that it was Laurence Olivier. He had come up to Granada to play King Lear.

'Oh,' I said, 'I'm so pleased to meet you. I've got a story to tell you.'

As we walked up the corridor I reminded him of how we had met 20 years before in his dressing room and how kind he had been.

He looked at me with tears in his eyes. 'What a wonderful story,' he said.

'*You* were wonderful,' I said. 'You gave me the will to go on and are responsible for me being here now.'

I always found Olivier inspirational. He was a very different actor from me – very intelligent, very technical. A lot of people found him cold, because he did work his performances out, but he was a superb actor and, in the theatre particularly, a great power.

In its own way *Coronation Street* has a type of power. Some people really take it to heart. When Ken left Deirdre and had an affair with Wendy Crozier, I was dropping my children off at school one morning when a mother pulled her child away, saying, 'Don't go near that man!' Apparently her husband had had an affair and she'd taken what I'd been doing on screen so personally that she believed I was like that in real life. Now in a way that's a compliment.

Ken is a very well-established character by now and the writers know exactly what he's like. There have only been only a couple of occasions in nearly 50 years when something in the script has struck me as not being right. One was during the big Ken/Mike/Deirdre battle. Imagine that your wife has been having an affair with somebody and you're having a row about it in your own hallway when there's a knock at the door and the guy that she's having the affair with is there, right in front of you, saying, 'You all right, Deirdre, he's not bothering you?' and then you just stand there for a page of dialogue. When we came to the scene I said to the director, Brian Mills, 'Sorry, I just *cannot* do that.'

Brian was someone with whom I had always had a particularly good working relationship and he was open to ideas. He said, 'Well, what would you do?'

I said, 'Well, I'd go to hit him or something...'

'You can't do that because it's not followed on in the script.'

'All right,' I replied, 'well, let me attempt to hit him and let Deirdre slam the door.'

'Great, let's go for that.'

So we did the usual thing – quietly going through it, with the moves, getting the words in, making sure we knew what we were doing – and then Brian said, 'Right, let's go for it.'

We started off, but Anne Kirkbride, playing Deirdre, was far too slow for me, so I had to grab hold of her and slam her against the door, because I wasn't going to let Mike get a word out. She burst into tears and said, 'Oh, I didn't think it was going to be like that!' and I said, 'Well, it is,' and she cried, but still we carried on. And we got awards for that scene. It's one that is often shown on programmes of *Coronation Street* highlights. There was a lot of genuine frustration in that scene and it did work well.

On another occasion Ken had a baby by the hairdresser, Denise Black, and he was very protective of him. She'd gone off with another man and left the baby behind, and Ken wouldn't have anything to do with her. Then we had a script where he went out one night and had a babysitter in and she rang and said she'd come with her boyfriend to take the baby. And from having been so strongly protective earlier, Ken turned up and in one short scene said to her, 'OK, just take him, take him.' As an actor I thought that was improbable. I couldn't believe Ken would do that, I am after all his guardian and I will fight for him when I have to.

The director said, 'This is the way they want it to happen and they want Ken to rationalize that if he lets the boy go he stands a better chance of getting him back.'

I found it difficult to play. I had to ratchet myself down, literally in a few paragraphs, from wanting at all costs to hold on to this child to saying, 'Take him.' That was difficult. Normally the writers are brilliant, but on that occasion they were in a hurry to get the situation changed. Such moments are rare, however.

It's always interesting to play big emotional scenes. When you do, you're releasing adrenaline, just as if it were for real. I don't like that too much. Particularly when I have to lose my temper as Ken. It'll never stop, though, not with Blanche and Deirdre around!

Rows make good television. But I learned from Dr Maugham that you could be very hard on someone but not lose your temper. There's an important difference. Losing your temper means exactly that – you're out of balance, you've lost yourself, and you've gone. Emotion has taken over. Reason is out of the window and so is everything else. When somebody loses their temper it's actually quite frightening because they are out of control and that can lead to all sorts of awful things. When I see somebody who is really angry it disturbs me because you can see how far removed they are from their true self, their spiritual self. They've let the animal take over. When you fall into anger, you're relinquishing your higher eternal self and letting your emotional temporary self take over. Taken to extremes, that anger causes all the violence, war and abuse in the world. So with Ken now I try to take the view that he may *seem* to lose his temper but he's actually giving someone what he thinks they need – with love. I try to be like that myself. Of course, we're all imperfect, but I try to look at it from that perspective.

In the early days of *Coronation Street* we were restrained from doing other shows in order to keep our characters believable, but now we are allowed – sometimes encouraged – to appear on different shows.

I have done a fair number of other shows and they can be very enjoyable. On *Stars in Their Eyes*, I went on as Perry Como and sang 'Catch a Falling Star'. I can't sing, but I managed to get away with that very simple song in a very laid-back manner. That was a big achievement for me, possibly the highlight of my lamentable musical career – even though I was terrified, just as Sara was. The truth is, I would love to be a singer, I think it must be the most wonderful thing in the world to get up there – as Al Jolson did – and grip an audience with beautiful music, but sadly that's a talent I don't have.

As I said earlier, if I'm asked to do something and I really feel I can't, I'll always say yes. By accepting a challenge you move yourself forward. You don't accept your limitations.

I was asked to speak at the Oxford Union once and I was really terrified because I'm not an intellectual at all. The topic for debate was: 'Will Margaret Thatcher's legacy be a good one or not?' This was when she was still in power, and having met her on a number of occasions I knew she was not a woman out to win popularity polls but a sincere conviction politician. It was quite a mixed audience, but there was some incredible hostility towards Mrs Thatcher and a very powerful left-wing girl really attacked me, saying, 'You climbed up on the backs of the workers!'

I was quite amazed to hear all this. I could understand her viewpoint in a way, because prior to the formation of trades unions, workers were treated extremely badly and still are in many ways. But I hadn't been part of it and I hadn't climbed up on the back of anybody. I hadn't inherited anything and had earned all the money I had off my own bat, so I was slightly upset, but curious also. Yes, I had a good education but why should that be held against me? It was the first time I'd come across someone who, while sincere, seemed totally unable to see anyone else's point of view.

In fact I always felt, right from the beginning, that I shouldn't have to turn to my parents for anything. I wanted to fend for myself, to do my own thing, earn my own money, make my own career. I was never one for running back home or wanting money from my parents, though there were times when I desperately needed it because I always lived beyond my means – the pay you get as an actor in a soap is not that of a big-selling recording star or even a headlining comedian and yet we are regarded as being in that category and expected to live up to it. The pay simply isn't sufficient to finance the life-style that we are believed to maintain and I'm not talking super-extravagance here. We have a house in Abersoch, North Wales, and we like an occasional bottle of champagne, but that's it. Mind you, our daughter's love of keeping horses did stretch the budget at one time.

My parents worked hard and then enjoyed their retirement. Uncle John died of lung cancer in 1975, at the age of 70. Although my father had diabetes, he still managed to enjoy life, but then he got bowel cancer when he was 82 years old. He chose to stay at home and be nursed by the Royal Alexandra nurses, who were wonderful, rather than go into hospital.

As he lay dying I tried to talk to him about spiritual matters, but he never wanted to discuss such things. A kind and loving man, he would talk about the family but he didn't want to know anything about what happened after death. He stayed like that right up to the end. That didn't hurt because I always wanted to be helpful to him; if it wasn't going to be, then it obviously wasn't right to pursue it.

He actually died of pneumonia. They call it 'the old man's friend'. I remember his heavy breathing. Then suddenly its pattern changed and then stopped. And that was it, he had passed.

My mother went on to be 95. I don't know what she died of in the end. She was very independent, living on her own right up to about the age of 93. Then she fell and broke her hip and that really did for her, she had to go into a home. I actually got to know her better then. I used to visit her there and we laughed about a lot of things.

Finally she went into a sort of coma. I remember going to see her once and she was lying there as if she was asleep, but her eyes were open. The nursing staff got a light and shone it across her eyes, but there was no response. In the end she just went to sleep. She died of old age, I suppose.

My mother was a great character and had real strength. Sara used to say my voice always changed when I spoke to her on the phone, that I was on guard. Possibly I was. I knew my mother had really made the most of her life. She had had no education as such and had left school at 14, but she had gone on to get a diploma in drama and become a magistrate and a director of the Townswomen's Guild drama group. She had done well, and I think I recognized that. I always wanted to please her.

I had very good parents and I hope that in turn my own children do not find me that bad, really. Just over a year after the death of Edwina, Sara and I had a son, William. The hurt of Edwina's loss was unbelievable and I wasn't sure whether we should have another child but William's arrival turned out to be a wonderful thing, a very happy event. As the children grew up we found ourselves involved in a great many activities, including horse-riding, as Verity became an excellent rider and competed very successfully with the British Show Pony Society. With family activities, sport, charity events, my glittering singing career and of course the drama of Ken and Deirdre's marriage, life was very full both on and off the Street.

CHAPTER 14

The Spiritual Path

'Align yourself with the consciousness of the soul.'

All this time I was continuing my search for answers to all the great questions of life. The great joy about being in touch with your spiritual self is that you do get answers. Seek and ye shall find, as it says in the Bible. So often I have put out a questioning thought and have received the reply with a wonderful feeling of excitement. It's like getting a long-awaited letter. The answer is not always what you expect, but you know without doubt that it is the answer.

I work my way forward by putting things to the test of experience. This is often a mental or an emotional test, a very personal test, where you receive the evidence to your own satisfaction. But your own satisfaction is what counts. It's only through personal experience that you really learn. Eventually, you just *know* when something is right. There are things that strike chords, like musical chords, and you know that they are true.

Learning in this personal way does mean, however, that you cannot prove to other people what you yourself know. I find that very frustrating. But of course ultimately it's quite right, because if you could just prove spiritual truths, people wouldn't develop in the correct way. You have to grow slowly and gradually. Every journey is totally individual and we each have to experience the events that we need to experience and overcome the difficulties we need to overcome, and that's how we move forward.

I don't think it's a gradual progression; I think we go along in fits and starts. Some incarnations we waste. We load ourselves up with too much to do and then don't make much progress. We never quite go back-wards, because a soul that's reached a certain level of consciousness and worth won't lose that, but we can take on too much in an incarnation and get sidetracked. Some incarnations zoom along wonderfully and you fulfil your destiny and your soul purpose and you go back and everyone says, 'Well done!' Others don't work out well at all. There's never any judgemental criticism or punishment in the spiritual realms, so when that happens people will just say, 'Well, never mind, you did your best but you overloaded yourself a bit there. Maybe next time don't set yourself such a big challenge.' But at the end of the day it'll be your decision as to what your destiny is.

> *'Lessons refused or neglected in one stage are presented in a far more difficult form in the next.'*

In every incarnation we have to try to overcome the lower self, and this has many aspects, not all of them bad. These aspects combine to form the personality, for good or ill, and until we are able go beyond it, the strongest of these will determine the type of person we are.

For the majority of men the desire for sex can be the strongest motivator, whereas in women it can be the need for security, which often manifests as the desire for money. The strongest desire will continue to mould the personality until either it is brought under control or the consciousness is raised to a higher level.

If one desire is brought under control, then the next strongest aspect will take over, and so on until all desire is controlled. That is when the lower self has been tamed. The higher self has no desire other than oneness with God.

> *'Spirit is master and matter is the servant.*
> *Let the spirit show its mastery.'*

There is a big difference between controlling and suppressing a desire. Suppressing a desire is putting a lid on a pan of boiling water: it has to erupt. Controlling a desire is having the power to move it into a higher channel and turn it into something good. Ridding yourself of a particularly strong desire has been described as like 'being un-chained from a lunatic'. It brings an incred-ible sense of peace.

Everyone is involved in this infinite process and we will all be given the environ-ment and circumstances that we need to help us progress on our spiritual journey.

Essentially we are all gods in the making. In our hearts there is a light that shines brightly. This is the part of God that is ours, or, shall we say, the part of us that is God.

This light is undeveloped and our soul is the vehicle that will carry it to maturity.

> *'The holy grail is that ever burning flame that shines in your heart.'*

This light covers itself in cloaks or bodies to take it on the journey of growth. Its first covering is the spirit body. This is then covered by the mental body, then the emotional body and then the etheric body. The etheric body is the exact replica of the physical body into which the soul will incarnate. When the spirit body is fully developed, all the other bodies will have served their purpose and been discarded.

The first body to be discarded is the physical body. What we call death is in fact the release of the other bodies, the bodies of higher vibration. As each body is discarded the soul rises to higher and higher levels until it reaches the level of pure spirit. From pure spirit we came and to pure spirit we return, but as an evolved being.

In the meantime life on Earth isn't easy for any of us and when you think of all the violence and hatred there are in the world, you can understand how a lot of people say, 'How can there be a God?'

To understand it, you have to think of the situation we are in. God has created a place for us to learn in and part of the process is that we are closed off from our true selves, so we feel we're alone, and we're given free will, because the point is that we have to battle on our own and work through our own development. As we go through it, during many incarnations, learning to discriminate between good and evil and right and wrong and to take responsibility, we inevitably do bad things because that's what the lower self wants. And that is where all the evil in the world has come from. We have created it through our desire for power and wealth and through the expression of our lust and anger.

That is all part of our lower nature and God gave us free will so that we could learn to overcome it. Now, He's not going to give free will on the one hand and then intervene. So the world is full of evil. But if it didn't exist, how could we learn the difference between good and evil?

God is often blamed for the evil here, but the real question is not how come He allows the suffering but how come *we* allow it? It can be very hard for us to accept the fact that it is us who are responsible for all the suffering.

'All the evil in the world has been caused by man's free will serving his baser self.'

Also, until we have total conscious control over ourselves, we have to go through suffering in order to learn from it. It would be nice if there were a way for us to grow without such suffering, but it's really the quickest way. It isn't easy for us to understand, and even though I'm now giving an explanation of it there are still certain circumstances, for instance when a loving family is totally devastated by some awful disease, when it just doesn't make sense to me. Life can seem very unfair. But that's because when we're here we only have a limited perspective. It's only when we get to our real home in the spiritual realms and look back that we get a true understanding of why we had to go through a certain set of circumstances. Then all is revealed.

In the spiritual realms we have a full understanding that there is an absolute deity – infinite love, infinite power, infinite wisdom – and that we are all part of it, but for our development at the stage we are at, as independent beings with free will we need to be put into the material world. It's a theatrical creation, in a sense. 'All the world's a stage,' as Shakespeare wrote. But while we're here we need to believe in it and live it fully. It's method acting taken to extremes. It can be painful, but at the end of the day it's a process that we've chosen to go through to overcome fear and desire and move on spiritually.

And ultimately, all the evil in the world will be dispersed and there will only be love. Love, always love.

> 'Know full well that love is the strongest power in any world in any condition.'

In the meantime help is always available if we ask for it. When you are feeling particularly down, just try asking for help, perhaps each night as you go to bed, and you will get a result – as long as you're not asking for the winning lottery numbers or some other materialistic thing, that is! Even then God will always answer your prayers in some way. It's just that more often than not what you're asking for isn't right for you and your destiny or you're not able to receive it at that time. But if you send out a prayer, it will be answered in some way. Then it's up to you whether you can receive it or accept it.

I know this works, because I've tried it. Once, quite some time ago, I was feeling a bit down. It didn't relate to anything particularly, but I was feeling low and I wanted to feel loved. So I asked to experience the love of God. Then one day I was walking in the park and I saw a mother pushing a pram with a baby in it. She was looking lovingly at the baby and the baby was looking lovingly at her. And I just burst into tears. The beauty of that mother! I felt tremendous love for her. And for the baby! And then I switched on the news and saw people starving in Ethiopia and again I wanted to cry. I felt so much love for them that it was almost unbearable. For the next few days, wherever I looked, whomever I saw, it was the same thing. I thought, *What's going on?*

What was happening was that I was feeling the love of God. He loves us, all of us. So I was loving other people, not *being* loved, as I thought it would be. I was just looking at life and loving everyone. It was almost unbearable to see some of the suffering, but lovely to see the happiness. And so I had the answer to my request to experience the love of God.

Ultimately, we are all one with God and the purpose of a religion is to bring us to a closer understanding of this. Tragically, quite the opposite has often been the case. In most religions a priesthood has set itself up as an intermediary between God and His people. But being ordained does not make anyone nearer to God. Neither does being well versed in theology. Closeness to God is dependent upon the state of a person's being, upon their individual worth. A simple man who loves those around him and goes peacefully about his duties can be more spiritual than a high-ranking priest.

Initially religious leaders arrive from the spiritual realms in a great burst of light and love. They have a direct contact with the divine source and are here to give out wonderful spiritual messages to humanity. Jesus came to give the message of love; Buddha came to give the message of enlightenment; Mohammed, I believe, came to teach courage. Each of the great teachers had a lesson for their people at that time.

The tragedy is, once these teachers go, the people left behind try to encapsulate their teachings and end up locking them into a rigid form. Then dogma is created, which is the deadening and divisive aspect of all religions. Ceremonies, rituals and extended teachings become the religion and they gradually move further and further away from the original message. So religions actually hinder the search for truth. They're just made up of empty ritual and people trying desperately to hang on to what they think are the great teachings of their original leader. But by that stage it's inevitable that the teachings have become distorted. The words of Jesus, for example, have been so distorted over the last 2,000 years. He didn't want a church, he just wanted people to love one another. And his was the greatest sacrifice – he's probably the most highly evolved spiritual being we know who has ever incarnated.

'Jesus had reached such a state of grace and purity that he could manifest the Christ principle of divine love.'

Jesus did not want hierarchy and ceremony but his simple message – 'Love one another as I love you' – to be understood and lived. He didn't want to be worshipped as God. He was indeed the son of God, as are we all, but he did not die so that our sins would be forgiven; instead he came to show us the way to the kingdom of God through retribution, forgiveness, love and service to others. 'I am the way, the truth and the life.'

Unfortunately Christianity has strayed so far from its simple origins that I feel it may have to suffer a complete breakdown before the true teachings can re-emerge. It has already fallen in influence and popularity. But Jesus is a great teacher and still loves us dearly and works in the heavenly realms on behalf of us all.

I was brought up in the Church of England and I still call myself Church of England, but I go back and forth in my attitude towards it. So many people who are in it are loving and well-intentioned and sincere in their beliefs, but I can't fully accept its teachings. I feel that what it does is take certain spiritual truths that it does understand and try to encapsulate them into doctrine. Well, spirit can never be encapsulated and held – spirit is free and open and loving and different for different people.

This is another reason why people are falling away from Christianity, because the consciousness of the human race is rising all the time and a lot of the Christian doctrine was really more suitable for people of another age, people who were illiterate or very poorly educated. The height of the Church's power was in the Dark Ages and it hasn't moved forward since then.

It's sad when you see individuals within the Church who are wrestling with their own faith, striving to understand and seeking the truth, but who aren't being helped by the teachings that they have been given.

'Theology emanates from the mind of humans. Thus revelation always must take priority over theology.'

Christianity has done a lot of good in many ways, but it's now not teaching primarily what it should be teaching. Splitting into different churches and sects hasn't helped. Nowadays, however, there is a strong ecumenical movement and some of the top people are showing a real willingness to bridge the divide and I'm still optimistic that they can.

Where I really part company with Christianity is over their lack of understanding about the spiritual realms and life after death. Not everyone in the Spiritualist Church and the various mystical movements agrees with reincarnation. But at least, as Peggy Kennard was always quoting to me, what esoteric writings say is, 'Never accept anything that offends your reason.' Now if you go to a Christian service and think rationally about what you're listening to and saying, half of it will offend your reason.

'There is only one religion, the religion of the living God.'

Atheists say that God doesn't exist, that He is man-made. They go about 'proving' their case by debunking religion and in that sense they are right because religions are man-made but that has nothing to do with the existence of God. Man with his theology has strayed from the truth and if people cannot accept theology they think they cannot accept God. Some religions are as far from the truth as atheism itself. But God does exist and you will find Him in every aspect of nature and within yourself. You do not need theology or religion; speak to your own soul – that is your point of contact with God.

I wanted to ensure that my own children had a spiritual awareness but weren't hampered by religious dogma or the fear of death that I grew up with. Verity and William had the lackadaisical easy-going Church of England take-or-leave-it side of religious education and we were never churchgoers apart from weddings, christenings and so on. There was no particularly strong religious element at all in their upbringing, but when they were in their late teens I gave them a short text I had written called 'A Gift of Understanding' (see page 361). They also heard me read it out in Manchester Cathedral one Christmas morning. It was really just a starting point for them.

Since then we have had the odd little conversation about spiritual things, but I do believe you shouldn't try and impose anything on people. When they're ready, they'll ask, and that's when you need to have the reply ready. At the moment neither of them has any particular interest in such matters. But they do know how I see things and they do refer to my views from time to time and seem to be in tune, as far as I see it, with them. It will be up to them at some point in their lives, if they wish, to go deeper.

My son from my first marriage, Linus, found his own way. He follows Andrew Cohen, who teaches a spiritual path that he calls Evolutionary Enlightenment. The focus is on the actual process of enlightenment and liberation, and it has benefited Linus tremendously. We email quite a lot and have great talks on the subject. He's following his own interests and rightfully learning a lot in the process because we should all choose one of the many different paths that best suits us.

This is why you should never condemn anything. However it may seem to you, if someone is improving as a result of it and gaining more knowledge about themselves spiritually, then it's good. It might not be for you, but don't dismiss it. The danger is when the ego gets involved and people say, 'My way is right. God only works through us.' It's horrendous that major religions actually teach that. And it is why they have committed so many atrocities in the name of God.

All the great religious teachers – Jesus, Mohammed, Buddha and so on – were essentially saying, 'Love one another. Work together.' And this is all that's needed. You don't need a church to be spiritual, you just need an understanding that there's one living God and you're part of it. We all are. We're all the same as God in essence, but not in degree. We're all little pieces of divine love trying to grow. We don't need dogma and ritual for that; all we need is to love and care and be compassionate.

I had the opportunity to speak on this when Douglas Baker, an esoteric philosopher, wrote to me asking me to open a lecture he was giving at the Festival of Mind, Body and Spirit in London. That would be in the late '80s. After that, he asked me to do some joint talks with him.

At first I wasn't very good. I was just reiterating what I'd read, rather than putting it across in my own way. And Dr Baker was very domineering. In a way we were like good cop/bad cop. He would do his talk and at the end people would ask questions and say, 'I don't understand,' and he'd tell them, 'Well, that's because you're not spiritual enough, you're not aware enough!' Sometimes he'd really have a go at them. Some people do need that, of course. And then I'd come along and try rather tentatively to say, 'Well, we're all trying to feel our way...' I don't know what people made of it!

Nevertheless, Dr Baker and I did several talks together. He was intellectually brilliant. He'd written hundreds of books, which he'd published himself, and he had an esoteric school at Essendon in Hertfordshire. He could talk about chakras and the technical side of spirituality, and working with him taught me a lot. It was through doing those talks that I realized how inadequate I was. I didn't really have the confidence to speak on such matters and I didn't have a rigorous enough approach; I didn't have enough of what he had. And that was my lesson.

After that it was quite a while before I did any more talks. But all the time I was reading, meditating and learning. It was only after I had done all those things that I had the great fortune to have my understanding moved forward by Peggy Kennard. As I've mentioned a couple of times, she saw me on the *Heaven & Earth* show and wrote me a letter. It was interesting and informative and I could tell she was someone with great understanding and great wisdom. I wrote back and we started a correspondence which grew and grew.

Peggy had a huge influence on me. At the time she was an elderly lady and had a muscular degenerative disorder. She could hardly get around and she knew she was going to go fairly soon, so she sent me a lot of her books as well as messages from spirit and lots of wonderful letters. That correspondence was a quantum leap for me; it improved me no end.

Peggy had had a tough life. Her husband

had died young. At one time she had been quite a mover in the Spiritualist Church, but then she had become disillusioned with that and left. But she understood the great truths and taught me a great deal. She helped others, too. She was a very strong lady. By the time she died, in 2005, she had vastly helped me to increase my understanding.

By then I was giving talks again. Suddenly, out of the blue – but I know it would have been planned at a higher level – Congleton Spiritualist Church had written asking if I'd give a talk. I've no idea how they knew I was interested in spiritual matters. Perhaps it was through one of the Douglas Baker talks. Probably it was for all the wrong reasons. But I accepted and it went on from there.

Now I nearly always feel really good when I'm giving a talk. I know there's help coming in. It's a lovely feeling. I've never felt the help of specific guides, but I do feel a love and warmth and light. If I am in a Spiritualist church, sometimes at the end a medium will say, 'Oh, I saw someone standing by you,' or 'I saw a great light around you,' but I just feel the love and the affection and the warmth. That's fine.

Before giving talks I always like a cup of

tea and half an hour on my own to prepare. I just sit quietly and feel calm and relaxed and hope I am becoming open to higher influences. Usually I can feel the warmth around me then. It doesn't always work that way, but some days it can feel wonderful and the talk can go really well.

When I talk at Spiritualist churches, most of the people there have a spiritual understanding, so you're preaching to the converted pretty well, although there are differences of opinion. Initially I used to be quite nervous about speaking elsewhere and being challenged. But that was down to my ego and I know I have to overcome that. I'm not here to preach or tell you how clever and wonderful I am with all my great knowledge – that's not what it's about. I'm here to learn. And being challenged in question-and-answer sessions can be so revealing. It can make me focus on a particular aspect of something I've said and really think it through.

I've found that if somebody asks a question, it's best to send love to that person. If the question is critical, which it often is, if you still love that person, instead of getting defensive and confrontational you are able to answer their question correctly, because through the love you discharge whatever caused their critical attitude, and you both learn something from it. It isn't actually done in a rational way, it's something that just happens if you're in the right frame of mind and *caring* about everyone you're talking to. If you want everyone – including yourself – to learn and move forward, then the right thing will happen.

'In life you get back what you give out.'

One group of people I talked to had all suffered the loss of a young child. Of course I was able to understand exactly what they were going through because of Edwina. Although they had grief in common, they had a wide range of views. There were of all religions, and none, in that room. After I had finished speaking, a silence descended on the room. I was thankful when someone broke it to say, 'That is the most beautiful thing I have ever heard.' Wonderful. Someone had been helped. Admittedly, a number of people remained silent and perhaps I had offended their reason, but later on they might have started to think. I might have planted a seed. You never know what's going on, really. All you can do is hope, love and

309

try to help.

A lot of people do have fixed views and aren't ready to accept anything else. That's fine. There's nothing you can do about it. You can't go around shaking them and saying, 'Now, look, you know, these things do happen!' It is an individual journey and you can't pass that on. Everyone has to do it for himself or herself. It's no good talking to someone who isn't ready – you'll meet hostility. They're just not ready. But life is such that sooner or later they will be presented with something that will make them think. That's how it works. You will always get whatever you need to move forward. You *can* choose to ignore it, of course, but then it will be presented in a more severe form, and so on and so on, until at some point you do think, *OK, there is something more going on here. I'd better have a look at it. What does all this mean?*

So instead of trying to 'convert' people, you just have to wait for them to come to you. It's a wonderful feeling when someone does, but it's also a tremendous responsibility. I've had quite a few people come up to me with questions and sometimes you get a tingle and you just know that they're really ready for answers. The danger is, you immediately want to quack out everything you think you understand in the hope that they'll get it. That's not the way. If somebody comes to you, what you have to do is to love them – I mean love in the spiritual sense. If someone comes and asks for help, you have to forget yourself, love them, listen to what they are saying and hope that you can drop the right words in or recommend the right book or point them in the right direction. The lower self will intrude; you'll think, *I know about all this, I can do this for them, I can teach them*. But wanting to be a teacher and all that ego stuff just stop everything, really. They get in everybody's way. So forget all that. If someone comes to you because they want to know something to take them forward, you have a responsibility to try to find what that is and give it to them. That's all.

Every time I go on *Heaven & Earth* or similar shows, I get letters. I got one the other day from a woman saying her husband had just died, she'd got an inflamed eye, she'd got an inflamed kidney, she had to go into hospital, she'd broken her toe and she'd lost all her money. It was a tale of woe from beginning to end. She had no one to turn to and just felt I was a sympathetic person. You have a responsibility when you get a letter like that and I try to do the best I can. It's very hard to start painting rosy spiritual pictures when someone's in the middle of physical and emotional pain. So I just tried to explain that her husband was close to her and would be sending her love and that if she could find some quiet time she would feel the love coming through and would find the strength to be brave and face her physical problems. Now, whether I rose to the occasion or not and whether that letter helped or not, I don't know, but I hope that somewhere in there there was something that gave her comfort.

You have to be careful when you do this, though, because a dependence can build up which isn't helpful to anyone. All of us have to stand on our own two feet. I never understood the phrase, 'The pupil dictates to the teacher' until I met Dr Maugham, but he would look at a pupil and see what they needed and then point them in their own direction. That was all the help he gave. The rest was up to them.

You can say all this, of course, and feel absolutely certain that you're making great spiritual progress and then something can come out of nowhere and smack you right in the face and you realize how far you really have to go. I'm afraid I experienced this is in a highly public and dramatic way.

CHAPTER 15

The Laws of Life

'Natural law is an immutable sequence of cause and effect. There are no chances, no coincidences, and the question of unfairness can never arise.'

There are no accidents in life, no coincidences. Everything that happens to us is something we've brought about or we're ready for or we need. If we are ready for something, we *will* get it. But our perception of ourselves is not the true one. We often think we need more, or less, or that something's not right for us, or not fair. But everything that is happening to us is happening for a reason and that reason is always good. However awful something is, it is something we need to go through and if we handle it correctly we'll come out wiser and stronger. It's *very* hard at times to accept this. But there *is* a reason, there's always a reason.

Probably our biggest battle here on Earth is facing and overcoming fear. All fear really stems from trying to hang on – to a set of circumstances, or your body, or your reputation, or to material things. It's pointless, really. If you know you are an eternal, immortal, spiritual being, who *cannot* be destroyed and who is loved and looked after, why are you frightened? But we all are. Basically we're frightened of losing our security and our comfort. And we're frightened of losing our life, because we've grown accustomed to it. Even when we have the understanding that we are immortal beings, it's very hard to contemplate giving up this life. You're attached to your body – with all its faults, you'd rather have it than not!

Fear is really only an emotion, but you can let it totally control you. I mean, look at all the funny irrational fears people have. I myself have claustrophobia. Even with all my understanding, I still don't like being confined. My body doesn't like it. Meditating has helped me to understand that it's just an emotion, an irrational fear that I know I should overcome, but it's still there.

I know I've got to work on that.

Another fear I obviously also had to work on, though I wasn't really aware of it at the time, was a fear of losing my reputation.

I was shown this in dramatic fashion in November 1990 when Ken Irwin, a *Sun* newspaper journalist who styled himself as 'the friend of the Street', wrote a series of articles 'celebrating' *Coronation Street*. This was somewhat ironic given that after the very first episode in 1960 he had predicted the show wouldn't last. More alarming was the fact that the first article, on Julie Goodyear, was full of unsubstantiated rumour and quite nasty in tone. It certainly wasn't a celebration. The next article was due to be about me.

'Within yourself lies the cause of whatever enters into your life.'

I had not given Mr Irwin an interview; in fact, I had been quite wary of the *Sun* ever since they had fabricated a nasty story about Jean Alexander and me three years before. I had complained to them at the time and asked for an apology to be printed. They had suggested we write a correction ourselves, which we did, but it was never printed, although we asked them several times, and in the end we just gave up.

Now I wondered what they were going to write about me. I don't normally buy the *Sun*, but that day I did. What I read was absolutely devastating. Without quoting any sources, Ken Irwin had written that I was hated by the cast, was a joke for the writers, was incompetent, had to be carried by other actors, for example in the famous Ken/Deirdre/Mike storyline, and had been nearly sacked more often than anyone else. He claimed this information came from unnamed 'insiders'. He also went back over all the stories about my life in the '60s, which was highly embarrassing, but at least there was some foundation for those, unlike his main allegation, which was that I was as boring and smug as Ken himself.

The 'Boring Barlow' tag had come from a dramatic scene where Ken had said to Deirdre, 'You think I'm boring, don't you?' It had stuck to Ken and I didn't much like it, in fact it was a pretty unpleasant thing to say even on a television programme, but at least it hadn't been applied to me personally. Until now, that is.

At the time the *Sun* had the largest readership in the country and I was horrified to think that millions of people were reading that article and perhaps believing every word. And it wasn't as if they wouldn't notice it – it was a massive centre-page spread.

When I got to work that day I headed straight for my dressing room. Although I knew for a fact that the cast didn't hate me and would actually have been very sympathetic, I just couldn't face seeing anyone.

I went to see Granada's company secretary, Alistair Mutch, who recommended that their lawyers, Goodman & Co., take a look at the article. Later they rang me to discuss it. They agreed that it was very defamatory and that I could probably sue for libel and win, but they didn't recommend that I should do so.

Granada's policy was never to back anyone in a libel case. Their view was that it could result in even more adverse publicity and with a trial by jury the outcome would always be uncertain. That was quite right, of course, but it still didn't seem fair to me.

'So what you're saying,' I said to the lawyer, 'is that the papers can libel anyone they like and be almost certain of getting away with it?'

He explained that most cases never came to court anyway because the costs were too high or the plaintiff was too frightened to go through the ordeal.

I was determined not to back down for either of these reasons. I engaged the services of the UK's leading libel lawyer, Peter Carter-Ruck.

Now I know this was totally the wrong approach. If someone's getting at you, you shouldn't be confrontational, you shouldn't try and justify yourself. You should try to forgive instead, or at least to move away from the situation. Otherwise, you're just acting out of pride or for financial reasons.

At the time I felt I was making a point. If I was successful, perhaps other people wouldn't have to suffer in the same way. But now I know it was just pride. I think I knew it then, though I didn't want to admit it, not even to myself. I was very hurt by the article, very hurt indeed. That was my ego being hit. You have to learn to disregard what happens to your ego, but instead I defended it and retaliated. If I had just let it all ride, people would have forgotten about it in a few days. As it was, I was in for a very bad time.

Initially, everything seemed promising. Peter Carter-Ruck gave my case an 80 per cent chance of success, which was the highest he ever gave to a libel case. I was very encouraged by that.

I went to meet him at his offices in Holborn and an extraordinary thing happened on my way back to Manchester. I was taking the train from Euston, but when I got there the train was in but the gates leading down to the platform were closed, so I joined the queue. I was reading a newspaper when I heard someone come up behind me and say, 'Hello.' It was Ken Irwin.

I couldn't believe it.

Was this strange meeting the universe throwing me a last chance to take a magnanimous view and shrug it all off? If so, I didn't take it.

I said, 'I was absolutely horrified by that article you wrote.'

'What article?'

'You know full well what article. I think it's the worst thing that's ever been written about me and I'm taking action.'

'Not against me, I hope.'

The effrontery of the man!

He muttered something like, 'Well, you know the sort of thing the papers want.'

That was the point. It was pure sensationalism.

'My solicitors will be dealing with that,' I said, and turned my back on him.

My solicitors were dealing with it, but there was a lot to do. We got some witness statements from the cast refuting the allegations that had been made. Amanda Barrie, Betty Driver, Johnny Briggs, Bill Waddington and Michael Le Vell were all prepared to testify on my behalf and I was really heartened by their support.

We wrote to the editor of the *Sun*, Kelvin McKenzie, offering him the chance to apologize and pay our costs, but he didn't reply.

The date for the court hearing was set for 29 October, 1991, almost a year after the publication of the article, and all this time the lawyers' fees were mounting up. I now realize that when you resort to the law all you are doing is paying people to argue for you. Really, you're just paying someone to do your dirty work for you. You just sit there while it all goes on around you and vast debts build up...

In September the *Sun* paid £25,000 into court. What this meant was that if I took that money, the defence would make an apology, the case wouldn't proceed and the *Sun* would pay my costs.

Peter Carter-Ruck and I both thought this wasn't enough, because the paper stood to make far more than that from the increased circulation that would follow from the publicity about the case. I didn't particularly mind how much I received in damages, but obviously the more I was awarded, the stronger the point I had made, so, on advice, I refused the money.

It was also explained to me that now the *Sun* had paid this money into court, if we were awarded damages above £25,000, that was fine, but if they were the same as or below that figure I would be liable to pay both sides' costs from the time the money was paid into court. This seemed a little worrying, but I was still pretty sure I would win.

The following month the *Sun* put another £25,000 into court, making £50,000 in total. So once again, on advice, I refused the offer, although this time I was a little nervous about doing so. The case proceeded.

With so many cast members due to speak in court, as well as writer Tom Elliott, producer Mervyn Watson and director Brian Mills, *Coronation Street*'s schedules were quite severely disrupted, but the Granada management was very supportive.

Sara, too, was absolutely brilliant and I was

incredibly grateful for that, especially as the counsel for the defence, Mr Eady, insisted upon asking the court to read the section of the article that I was *not* protesting about, which concerned my life in the '60s. That gave every tabloid a lot of fodder and diverted people's attention from the real issue, which was just what the *Sun* wanted.

The pressure was terrible. My pulse rate soared and remained high for weeks afterwards. I had thought I was prepared for the ordeal, but I wasn't. And it was even worse when I found every last detail splashed all over the newspapers day after day. The *Sun*'s article had been extremely unkind and wrong, there's no doubt about that, but somehow I found myself on trial instead.

An example of Ken Irwin's methods came to light when he gave his evidence. He had claimed that I had once given him an official interview. I knew I hadn't, but then he produced a transcript, followed by a cassette tape, and there I was, talking to him. I couldn't remember it at all and began to wonder if I was actually going mad.

Then I realized that the only time I'd ever spoken to him, apart from at Euston station, was at the opening of Stage One, a set that had been built especially for *Coronation*

Street. I had been representing the cast. After the launch and some questions from the press, I'd got some food from the buffet and walked round chatting to people, including Ken Irwin. But I was speaking on behalf of the company that day, not giving a personal interview. And I had no idea he had a hidden tape recorder.

On the witness stand he still insisted that I was hated by the cast, even though the newspaper itself had now apologized for the line containing those words, but he was unable to name any of them. Enough said.

The case had started on a Tuesday and by Friday afternoon the barristers were summing up, but there wasn't time for the judge's summing up and directions to the jury, so the trial was adjourned until the Monday. That weekend Sara and I were trapped in our hotel, unable to go out because of all the photographers hanging around. It was an incredibly tense time, not helped by the Sunday papers having a field day.

On the Monday morning the judge, Chief Justice Waterhouse, summed up very thoroughly, going through the whole case, and when he mentioned damages, he stressed that they should not be punitive. That worried me, because punitive damages were the point. A mere rap on the knuckles wouldn't stop the *Sun* from doing it all again to someone else.

The jury was out for about an hour and three-quarters and by that time I just wanted to go away and forget about the whole thing.

When the jury foreman returned and said they had found in my favour, though, my heart soared. It had all been worth it. Now those allegations were known to be false and were proven to be false. It had been proven that the *Sun* had libelled me. I had won.

But now came the big lesson. What damages had the jury awarded?

'Fifty thousand pounds.'

It was incredible. That was the exact sum that the *Sun* had paid into court, which meant that I was liable for all the costs – about £800,000 worth. And the jury didn't even know what money had been paid into court. It was an amazing coincidence. Only there are no coincidences, no mistakes. The laws are absolute. Now, when I look back, I can see karma at work. I was meant to be hit really hard, and I was.

At first it didn't seem so bad. My counsel immediately petitioned for me to be awarded costs and the judge obliged.

But the *Sun* continued to blacken my name. The very next day their front-page headline was, 'Roache demands £200,000.' That wasn't true at all, but it served to draw the public's attention away from the fact that the *Sun* had lost the case. It was also taken up by other newspapers, which portrayed me as being out for all I could get. It was very unpleasant to have to live through that.

Then the *Sun* launched an appeal. That wasn't heard for another year. By that time I had developed an ulcer and had to be taken into hospital. The stress was terrific.

I was beginning to hate every moment of the whole process. I would have loved to have just walked away. But by now there was an inevitability about it. I felt it was something I had to go through. It got to the point where I really began to feel karma at work and I just knew that things weren't going to go right, even though everyone said we couldn't lose, no way.

But we did. The panel of appeal ruled that if the amount paid into court was met by the damages, the plaintiff must pay the costs. That was the law. So I had to pay the original costs and the costs of the appeal as well. It seemed ruinous at the time but I was very well looked after – we were so well looked after – that in the event we didn't have to sell the marital home and the children were still able to go to their private schools.

It was a hard lesson learned. By acting out of pride and protecting my ego, I had brought incredible financial problems on myself – even though I had won the libel case!

At the time I wasn't even aware I needed the lesson. If I had been, perhaps it wouldn't have been such a big one. But you need hard lessons in order to develop. Difficult experiences are precious gifts. They give you the opportunity to go through the mill. You don't want to, of course, but if you do, you experience something, you learn a lot and you emerge better and stronger as a result.

Such experiences are karmic. You have chosen to go through them in order to discharge some negativity from the past and you move forward as a stronger person.

What would I have done now? Nothing! Articles like that are hurtful, but people soon forget. They move on, and so should you. You shouldn't react, you shouldn't respond, you should just try to understand and forgive. That was the lesson I needed to learn.

I think that in life if you have a conflict

with somebody you should always give a little more than you want to. If you do that you will find it helps discharge matters. You'll get a response and you will resolve things.

I'm not saying that you should surrender to something that is wrong, but you should have a good look at the problem and examine why it's there. Is there any pride, greed or other negative ingredient on your part? Remove that from yourself and then face up to your difficulties and be strong. And if you can just give that little bit more, even if it might hurt you a little, you'll find that most disputes will simply go away. It doesn't always work, but it's worth a try!

There should be no need to go to law. I know there are lots of genuine people in the legal profession, but my advice would be to go to the law for conveyancing or wills, but otherwise use your own judgement and come to terms with things yourself if you can.

Pride is a big enemy. And it comes in many guises. You have to watch out for it, because pride is the ego at work. The libel case was all down to pride, really. It was a great lesson. I just hope I don't ever have to go through anything like that ever again!

The aftermath lasted for ages – three or four years. There were bills that went way beyond what we could afford and we had huge financial problems. It got to a point where more lawyers were involved and insolvency people had to come in and it seemed a never-ending process. The lawyers were trying to sort everything out, but their fees were mounting up and the whole process was gaining a momentum of its own.

Suddenly one day I took back my own responsibility. I told the lawyers to stop acting on my behalf and I went to meet the people who were fighting me over the finances and we began to work things out. Slowly we came out of the cloud.

From this I also learned that if you tackle something in what you regard as the most difficult way, you'd get the best result. It may be embarrassing or hard, but wonderful things can happen. For me, the way forward became clear almost miraculously.

Never let other people fight your battles for you. If you're in a difficult situation, you've got to be realistic and face it head-on and deal with it yourself. If you actually are incapable of dealing with it yourself for some reason, perhaps because you lack the professional knowledge, there's no harm in seeking advice, but don't just shelter behind a group of people who might not really have your best interests at heart.

It's always best to experience things yourself, deal with things yourself, suffer the consequences if necessary and grow as a result.

In the end Sara and I were able to get back on an even keel financially. It took a long time, but we did it and Sara was a great support all the way through. We fought our way back.

The court case was a big watershed in my thinking. I had been seeking security in the material world and that wasn't right. I had been looking in the wrong place. There is no security in the material world. Everything is subject to decay and change. Everything, even the Earth, the sun, the whole universe.

The only permanence is your immortal state, your state of being, your soul. That is eternal. But it's the only thing that is. There's no security materially.

Once I realized that, I felt much easier and happier. If you're looking for something in the wrong place, it's frustrating and you always have a feeling that things aren't quite right. But the minute you realize that the only security, the only permanence, is your spiritual self, that's fine. Then you're walking down the right road. Then you can put your energy into what is meaningful and not waste your time and energy on the inevitable distress and failure.

It is liberating, totally liberating.

CHAPTER 16

Moving Forward

'The only thing in life that you can be sure of is change.'

Life goes on, always moving, always changing, and once I had stopped looking for permanence in the material world, I was much more at ease with it.

Coronation Street was an ever-present fixture, of course, but even the way we worked on it changed completely over time. In the early days we had rehearsals and run-throughs and technical run-throughs, so by the time we came to do it we really knew it. About ten years ago we started having three episodes a week and so the rehearsal time had to go because all the time available was needed for filming. Then about four or five years ago we went to five episodes a week. Now we've no rehearsal at all, there's no prompting and we have to be word-perfect. So we learn it at home, turn up, do it and go back home again.

Filming goes on from 8.00 in the morning until 7.30 at night six days a week. Saturday is the only guaranteed free day. Of course, none of us is filming all the time; the amount we do depends upon our involvement in the storyline. When we are heavily involved we can spend nearly 12 hours in the studio and then have to learn our lines at night. If you are in five episodes a week and in several scenes in each one, then all you do is work, sleep and work again. There's really no time for anything else. But nobody has that for too long. The cast is big and the load is spread.

We do get through an amazing amount of work. An 'A' feature film will probably record two minutes in a day but we'll record 20 minutes to half an hour, maybe more. It's a lot. Also, sometimes a great many actors are involved – big groups in the Rover's, party scenes – such scenes can mop up a lot of time. And then there are all the external shots in addition.

We get the scripts about ten days before filming, but we're usually working on something currently as well, so there are times when we seem to be permanently learning. It doesn't make it easy to plan the rest of your life. You usually know two or three months ahead how many episodes you are going to be in and therefore how busy you're going to be. But sometimes – just when you think you're in for a quiet week – it doesn't work out that way: along come post-shoots from the week that's gone and pre-shoots for the week that's ahead. Apart from fixed holidays – we each get five weeks a year – the scheduling can play havoc with such things as dental appointments and anniversary celebrations.

But the work's good and although this system is more intense, I prefer it, because if you have to get very emotional in a particular scene, you don't have time to rehearse it, you just do it, and the spontaneity pays off. If you have rehearsed something and worked on it over and over, what you do is recapture the initial feelings and act them out. That's how actors in the theatre can go through highly emotional stuff night after night and really not feel very much. They've got it down pat, they know how to do it, it's almost routine. But with us you get the real thing.

There is a good atmosphere at work and we all get on remarkably well, but most of us don't socialize. As soon as any of us has finished we are in the car and on the way home. That's understandable, given the intensity of our work. It's a friendly place to be, though, in spite of the pressure. There is a fair amount of fun.

We don't know a lot about each other's private lives, although everyone is supportive if one of us is in trouble or in need of help. As I've pointed out, the majority of the cast don't know about my interest in spiritual matters; it's not something I choose to talk about unless someone comes to me and broaches the subject. There are a few people with whom I can have interesting conversations, though. It's always a joy to me when someone wants to talk about these things and it is amazing how quickly a like mind is recognized.

'We are all eternal beings and, as such,
whether we know it or not,
we all love one another.'

Some weeks work takes up all my time and other weeks are less demanding. But generally speaking, *Coronation Street* is as near a nine-to-five job as you will get in this profession, and it does give me the chance to do other things.

When I was starting out, all I knew was I had to be an actor. People said, 'There are lots of very famous actors out of work,' and 'You're not a member of Equity,' and 'You know nothing about it.' That didn't matter. Nothing would stop me. You do have to be realistic, though. When my sons wanted to go into acting, I said, 'You've got to understand what it's going to be like – you've got to be able to take the rejection, and the work is hard.' Today I get lots of letters from people saying, 'I want to be an actor. How can I get on telly?' and I can see that all they really want is that moment of fame. That's no good. Forget it. Get on with something you're driven to do. You've got to go inside and find out what it is that you *really* want. That's the only way.

I not only wanted to be an actor, I needed to be one. But I remember being asked ages back, soon after I started my spiritual development, 'Do you think that this is compatible with the work that you do?' I got really worried about that. There was a time when I thought that maybe it wasn't. The thing with acting is, it's a real ego-trip business. I did wonder for a while whether I would have to give it up. But as time went on I realized that it could be a tool for good. I'm in a job that opens doors. I'm asked to give talks, I know, just because I'm on television. That's fine by me and I'm very happy if a lot of people come to the talks for that reason only. Maybe what I say will give them a glimmer of something that could be of interest and help to them. I think this could be part of my contribution to life – talking about these things to people who might not otherwise hear them. So fame has enabled me to sow seeds in people's minds.

By now I've got pretty philosophical about being well-known. I actually forget about it sometimes and it surprises me when someone says something. But the recognition factor is extraordinary. Cars on the motorway will suddenly start pulling in behind or in front, just to look at me driving! Sometimes I will go into a café for a quiet coffee and be faced with a busload of holidaymakers all clamouring for autographs. Occasionally it can be inconvenient, but usually it's very pleasant. People are very good. They can get quite protective, actually. A lot of them don't want to bother me. Sometimes if I'm walking down the street (not *the* Street) I won't be aware of anyone recognizing me at all and then my wife will say, 'Did you see those people? Once they had passed you they all turned round and went, "Did you see who that was?!"'

Fame doesn't mean a lot in terms of your state of being, of course. If you take it seriously and try to build on it too much in any way, it's dangerous. Fortunately I've never been in the position of really letting it go to my head. Possibly my background helped. It is hard for people who get it for a short time and it is taken away from them before they can adjust to it; it is also hard if you get it too young. The three years I had in repertory also helped to keep my feet on the ground. That was such a hard grind and I learned so much from my colleagues that there was no way I could get carried away!

My son Will has also had a break by going to university before going into acting; that has been his equivalent of my army career, in a way. He hasn't come to me for advice; he wants to do it all his own way. I don't get any feeling that he's following my footsteps, as he's very much his own person, and that's quite right. I hope he does well. I think he will.

My elder son, Linus, is already a very highly respected actor and I am very proud of his achievements. He did 15 years in the theatre with the Royal Shakespeare Company and the National Theatre, and then went out and did some great television and films. He played the title character in Antonia Bird's *Priest*, Batman's father in *Batman Begins* and Bob Longman in *Seaforth*. Yes, Linus has done some really great work (though sadly I must confess that I was not at any of his opening nights – we were not meeting in those fraught early days which, to this day, remains one of the big disappointments of my life). What most people in the UK don't know is that in America he played Bobby Kennedy in *RFK*, a TV dramatization of Bobby Kennedy's life. It was a great achievement for an English actor to play an American idol and he was nominated for a Golden Globe for it, to go along with his *Evening Standard* Best Actor award. The series hasn't been shown over here. I have no idea whether it will be. He recently played FBI Agent Andy Archer in *Kidnapped*, a major US mini-series that has been broadcast over here. His was a key role as it was revealed that he was the villain in the end. He also makes a lot of films, mainly in Canada, and he likes to go off to India to follow his spiritual interests. Having run along classical lines, Linus's career has worked out wonderfully well for him.

I'm truly delighted for his professional success but I am equally pleased that none of my children has gone through the terribly distressing drug problem that so many parents have to endure: I did a session recently at Styal women's prison and was astonished to learn that 60 per cent of them are inside for drugs-related crimes, although I did meet one woman who seemed proud of the fact that her offences related to beating up other women for a living! For £100 she would violently 'do' anyone. That would certainly have shocked Ken. When I asked her if she felt any remorse, she said, 'No, not at the time because it was just a way of life.' But she made it clear she wanted to change. I can't talk to people about spiritual matters in situations such as this, just to try and bring out the good that is in them somewhere – as it is in all of us.

In films, you have the luxury of time. Acting in television serials can be far more demanding, however, as you have to play the full range of emotions with precious little rehearsal. I have some dramatic scenes to play that are as good as you will find in any film. I am proud to be in *Coronation Street,* care very much about my performance and get great job satisfaction. I have no regrets. Of course I wonder sometimes what would have happened if I hadn't stayed in it, but you can always look back and say, 'What if?', can't you?

The Street gives me the security of having work and it imposes a discipline that's useful to me. You have to be ready for your scenes and in a fit state to play them. You can't be up until four o'clock in the morning partying and sniffing cocaine and drinking alcohol and then rise two hours later and come to work looking reasonable and knowing your lines. So there's quite a lot of discipline involved for all of us, which is not a bad thing. And I can be quite lazy, so it keeps me going!

Ken is a pretty easy-going sort of guy, which is fine; I wouldn't have liked to have played a nasty person for such a long time. When you're acting, as I mentioned earlier, you do release adrenaline and emotions appropriate to the moment, and I think playing, say, a serial killer for nearly 50 years would have been harmful to me. But Ken's a well-meaning sort of chap, an ex-teacher who wants to do right by the world, and he's always trying to keep the peace in his wonderfully dysfunctional family, so it's OK. I rarely have to play a scene where I feel that I am going to suffer. Though I do have to lose my temper rather a lot.

I remember when I was in the theatre doing a play a week, when we were doing a comedy there would definitely be a light, happy feel about the place and when we were doing a horrible murder there would be a certain darkness. Even though we were just acting – and to a large extent being incarnated into a physical body is acting – we did get affected by it to a certain extent.

Acting is interesting from that point of view. Of course, part of the enjoyment of it is being able to do things you're not able to do in real life. I had a big scene once where I had a row with Deirdre and I had to throw the table over with all the crockery on it, which was really enjoyable because it's not the sort of thing I would normally do. We only did it once, so no one really knew what was going to happen once the table had gone over, but it worked and it was really satisfying.

Acting is also quite a good profession for someone who wants to know about life, because taking on lots of different parts can give you great insight. And you have the ego challenge too. It gives the ego a great boost to have an audience laughing at your jokes and falling silent when you have your dramatic moments. Control of an audience is something actors have to do and it can be a very powerful thing. You have to be careful that you don't enjoy the control and manipulation too much. But most actors feel horribly inadequate anyway!

On television you don't get feedback from an audience, of course. Maybe one of your fellow actors will say something or the director will come back at the end and say, 'Yes, great, that was fine,' but you don't get the immediate impact of an audience, which is why you can only learn the craft – how to time a laugh, hold a pause or make people cry – by performing in front of a live audience. But I've no desire to go back to the theatre now. It takes so much effort. Theatre work is hard work both physically and mentally because your concentration has to be total, night after night. So I don't think you're going to get my King Lear. No, I've missed that!

There are still challenges at work, though. It's always interesting if a new character comes into your particular family or environment. It's quite refreshing, really, because you tend to be working with people you know and suddenly there's a new character to work with. We all enjoy it and welcome new people in. I always say, 'If you can work the tea machine, everything else will fall into place.'

Generally, we're a pretty happy group. There's no aggravation, no temperament. It can be quite intensive work, but I do enjoy it and I've no intention of stopping.

In addition to being a wonderful wife, Sara is also my manager – she has always been amazingly well organised and handled the financial side of things in addition to running the house so beautifully. But I'm delighted to report that her acting career is back on track now that the children are becoming independent. She's been in *Emmerdale* and *Cracker* and also appeared recently in *Coronation Street* playing Judge Alderman, the judge who sentenced Tracy Barlow (my screen daughter, of course) to 15 years' imprisonment for murder.

I've also been taking up one of my old pursuits recently: astrology. In addition to the column I do on the subject for the *Lancashire Magazine*, I'm also doing one for the *Yorkshire Magazine*, and there will soon be a third – the *Cheshire Magazine*. I also like to interview interesting celebrities for the magazines (as I mentioned earlier, I'm a director of the company that publishes them) and have just done one with Cliff Richard. Well, to be honest, it's not so much an interview as a chat. I call it 'A Conversation with...' Other interviewees have included Freddie Trueman, Russell Grant, the Bishop of Manchester, Betty Driver, Kate Ford, Gloria Hunniford, Harold Riley and Anne Kirkbride.

There is wonderful astrological software now that will do your chart and give you the interpretation, but I find that just having an ephemeris, looking at the signs and seeing where the planets are is more helpful to me than having software churning something out. I don't have to draw up a chart for the sun-sign column, I just have to see where the planets are placed, know what the ruling planet of each sign is doing and what is aspecting it, and take it from there. It is not possible to be specific, as in an individual chart, but I can get a general view and relate it to some philosophy.

At first I was quite rusty and it took a while to get back into it. Still, Sara read my columns and thought they sounded OK. She said, 'It sounds as though you know what you're talking about.' One day I suddenly found myself reading my own!

Overall, astrology can be a useful tool and it can lead to the realization of great truths. A lot of people who are not interested in spiritual matters will still read their daily horoscopes. That can be a good starting point.

We're all part of a living, moving cosmos and are changing with it and within it. Astrology can show this.

Despite the sometimes-intensive demands of all my work, every morning I try to remember that I'm an eternal being and to be grateful for the infinite love that is a part of us all. And then I arrive at the studios at 7 o'clock and go through a whole load of scenes where I'm screaming and shouting!

There is a reason for this, of course. In a way, it's a test. It's easy to maintain a spiritual focus if you are sitting meditating in a monastery and nothing is disturbing you. But if you can keep that meditative calm or that understanding of your spiritual nature while actively participating in the material world, then it's stronger – it's for real.

> *'Every morning lean your arm upon the windowsill of heaven and gaze upon your God. Then, with this vision in your heart, turn strong to meet the day.'*

Ideally, you should meditate at a fixed time each day – say, dawn or dusk – and in the same place, because then that will be a little pocket of peace for you. As I've mentioned, my lifestyle is such that this isn't possible, and I'm afraid I'm not a creature of habit either, so I just meditate when I can, but I like to do it in my dressing room at work and in my conservatory at home.

I also try to hold a thought or phrase in my mind, perhaps something that I've been reading, and ponder on it. One I've been thinking about recently is, 'All the bad experiences are precious gifts.' When I do this I find that suddenly during the day all the words seem to expand and each word becomes greater and more important. And afterwards I am able to see with a different perspective.

A little while ago I was holding the thought, 'Help me to realize my oneness

with the infinite love,' and suddenly 'oneness' became almost solid, as if it had form.
It was actually *there*. You could weigh it! And
'realize' – what is to 'realize', to make real,
to fully absorb, to become? It's to know it
completely. And to realize *the infinite love!*
What an amazing thought.

If you hold something in your mind in this
way, you go more and more deeply into it
and eventually begin to *become* it. Over time
you assimilate it completely, it becomes part
of you, and then you can move on and hold
another thought. It's a bit like learning golf,
really, or cricket – you learn a technique and
then after a while you do it automatically
and move on to something else.

I once put some of my favourite thoughts
together and called them 'A Prayer of
Intention':

A Prayer of Intention

Ever-present all-loving Father, strengthen me
  in my intention
To be whole,
To align myself consciously with my soul,
To remember I am immortal,
To feel in my heart the reality of your loving
  presence,

To retain the power entrusted to me,
To rejoice in being eternal,
To bring my body into harmony with the whole
And thus to realize my oneness with the infinite
  love.

Each line of this prayer can be used for deep thought and meditation. I have found it helps greatly in expanding understanding.

Another good phrase to hold in your mind is, 'Love, always love.' That was how one of the spirit messages I got from Edwina, through Peggy Kennard, ended. If you think about it, it's amazing. Life is love, it's what it's all about – and it's *always* there. Love, always love! Love is the dynamic of life. Love is the life force. Life is love. All we have to do is release it, but sadly we are better at obscuring it.

I have some rose bushes at home. There are five of them. I've had them for four or five years. One is called 'Love', another is 'Always', a third is 'Light' and the others are 'Friendship' and 'Infinite'. Most are light pink and one is a deep red, but they've all got a lovely fragrance. They are just by my front door and every morning when I get into my car, I look at them and, especially through the winter, I send love down to their roots and say to them: *Use this love to build your reserves so that you can fully manifest your beauty.*

I thought that giving them love like that would really help them to flourish, but one day I looked at them and saw that they were covered in greenfly!

At first I was horrified by this, and disappointed too, because I thought it showed my loving thoughts had been ineffectual, but then I thought, *Hang on, what this means is it's no use just going about thinking, 'Love, love, love!' because we're in a material world and we've got to deal with the greenfly of this world.* I realized I was looking after the rose bushes spiritually but I wasn't looking after them materially, and when you're here on Earth you have to do both. So that was a lesson. I had to deal with the greenfly. I did and now the roses are blooming gloriously.

I do like to do a bit of gardening. I'm not a good gardener and I can't name flowers, but I like to see lovely things. And everything is alive, even rocks; everything has a spirit. Sometimes I'll be sending love to the rose bushes and I'll suddenly think, *Oh, I'm forgetting about the rest of the garden!* and decide to send love to the whole lot. Then I'll extend it further and send love to the cats and the dogs. And then I'll begin to think about the world and all the places that so desperately need help. This is something we can all do – start with sending love to something close by and then extend it to the whole world. It doesn't matter where you start. Just do it, it is greatly needed. It is not a pious, sanctimonious or even humourless thing to do; it can be a lot of fun, so enjoy it. And don't forget all those in other realms.

You do have to be a little careful sometimes, though. I remember Dr Maugham once said, 'Try giving a smile to strangers.' I mean, nowadays you do have to be a little wary, but don't let that stop you. You can make someone's day.

In a way, spiritual development requires constant vigilance. The material world will always provide distractions, usually through desire and fear. Fear is one of the biggest obstacles, as it blocks the channels of help, and desire will try to keep you occupied. This doesn't mean that you can't enjoy yourself, but you must never forget that you are a spiritual being. You don't suddenly become a spiritual being when you die, you are a spiritual being now. You are in this world, but not of it. The body is the temple of the Spirit. Yes, of course you should enjoy yourself, and the body needs looking after. Just remember the poor old passenger!

What you are is a little piece of God. God is infinite wisdom, infinite power and infinite love and is always growing and moving forward. So you could say God spins off little bits of Himself, tiny little pieces of innocent, immature love with a desire to grow and a desire for knowledge and a desire to love. Each piece will then start to go through certain processes. It'll be granite, it'll be stone, it'll be vegetation, it'll pass through the animal kingdom. Initially, according to my understanding, it will grow as part of a group until it reaches a point where it is able to realize its own individuality, which is when it will enter the human chain. It will come in at a raw, unrefined level to start with and gradually progress until it fully realizes its eternal spiritual self. And then it won't need to come here any more and it will carry on developing in the spiritual realms. Roughly speaking, that's the evolution, as I see it, of an individual soul.

'Does a man remember being a lion? Does a lion remember being a rose? Does a rose remember being granite?'

Ultimately, we are all responsible for taking our own little bit of spirit, God, divine love, up to a level where it will become consciously part of everything once more. Essentially, we all go out from the one, become the many and then come back. It's the story of the Prodigal Son, really. We all have to leave home and have all sorts of experiences in order to grow. We have to make mistakes, because that's how we learn. If we put our hand in the fire, it burns and we don't do that again. So our mistakes can help us to learn quite quickly. God is a constantly growing being and we are the growing points.

Also, as we develop it is a natural law that we should take what we learn and give it back out to others. Sometimes I think you can get to a point where if you don't give out you won't learn any more. A bucket can't receive more water from the well until it has been emptied.

When you fully realize that we are all spiritual beings and all part of one great whole, you also know that by harming another you harm yourself. If more people were aware of this we might finally have peace on Earth. Obviously we've a long way to go!

When you look around, it might seem as though no progress is being made at all. But the desire to move forward is always there. Whether you are incarnated or not, you never stagnate. Nothing stays still. Creation is always moving forward and we are always moving with it. If we don't do it consciously, we will be nudged forward, either by intuition or by suffering.

'Every atom of your being is a shining jewel.'

So what is the best way to advance? It's easy to become confused. You might think, *Should I go and join a monastery? Should I go out and help people?* Or in my case, *Should I carry on acting?* Dr Maugham used to say, 'Tackle the task in hand.' It might be cleaning your teeth. But whatever it is, do it, and do it fully. Don't get distracted. Each of us is responsible for our own development, so it is up to us to concern ourselves with the tasks that are presented to us and deal with them to the best of our ability. If you give your attention to whatever it is you are doing, however menial that task is, you are moving forward in the right way.

'We show forth the divinity within ourselves simply by the way we live.

Also, because we are all at different stages of development, it is pointless to compare yourself with others. You do not know where they are in the process of unfolding their spirit. Sometimes you will see someone who has behaved badly and knowingly harmed others and yet has all the material trappings of success. There is no need to be envious or resentful of that person. At some point they will have to pay the price, and envy only harms the person who harbours it, making them bitter and resentful.

If someone is harming you and making your life difficult, it may seem natural to hate them and be unforgiving and want revenge, but all these things are bad for you and will hold back your progress. Once you realize that the person who is behaving so badly is in need of help, you will also realize that the only way to give that help is to love them. That is the most effective way of changing their behaviour and it also frees you from hate and bitterness.

If someone has done something terrible to you, they will suffer the consequences. Whether you forgive them or not has no bearing on what will happen to them. Come what may, they will have to learn the lesson. So holding on to resentment only harms you. Forgiveness, on the other hand, releases you. It gives you freedom. Learning to forgive is one of the great lessons.

Basically, what we need to do is really quite simple – we need to find peace in ourselves and radiate love. This is the answer to everything. When we give off anger and other forms of negative energy, it just pollutes the world and at some point it has to be cleansed. Love is like a disinfectant – it cleans it all up. If every human being on this planet could get peace in their heart and radiate love, in an instant all the hate and violence would disappear and the Earth would be a paradise. In fact, there would be no point coming here – we wouldn't learn from it!

We are learning, though, and more people than ever before are understanding the spiritual nature of life and love and service. Ahead of us there lies a glorious new age, but we won't get there easily. There is a cleansing process to go through first. We've been through it before. Thousands of years ago, during the civilizations of Lemuria and

Atlantis, we reached a point where the world was so clogged up with bad thinking that all that energy had to burst like a big boil and the Earth had to be renewed and reborn. Everything comes in great cycles like this, including human epochs.

We can see now that we're approaching the end of one era and the birth of another. How that transition is managed is to a large extent up to how we behave. If enough people become good and pure and send out positive thoughts, it will be easier for us all. There may well be major climate change to contend with and the Earth may even shift on its axis, but it will not be destroyed. It is an important school and it will be renewed. There will be local devastation, but humanity will continue to exist.

This may sound alarming, but by making peace in our hearts and sending out prayers to Mother Earth and to all of humanity, we can modify these events. If we realize that every human being is a spiritual being and should be loved as a brother or a sister, we can bring peace to the planet and give humanity a greater chance of survival.

The Earth is known to be the planet of sorrow. It's a schoolroom, and it's a tough schoolroom, but it has to be. You can't have

355

all the exams made easy for you. That won't help you to learn. You will only improve if you go through some pretty tough training now and then. In a way, we're in a spiritual boot camp. But just as army training is really tough, later, when you look back, you respect and understand the process, so life on Earth is of great benefit to us all. And we chose to be here.

Everything is moving forward in the way that it should. Nothing is accidental. Everything is meant to be.

Epilogue

'Love solves everything. In the end there is only love.'

I have been on a journey of spiritual discovery for over 35 years. It has been a steep and rocky path. It is only by looking back that I am aware of any progress, and there is always the next mountain to climb, so there is never time for any complacency. However, when I think back to the self-indulgent days of the '60s, I am aware of some improvement. I only wish it had been greater and quicker. But this is a journey that cannot be rushed. Truths are revealed as the consciousness is raised, and then comes the ability to accept them. This takes time, but the journey is eternal.

Along the way we may ask for direct guidance from our soul and eagerly await this contact, but when we do receive it, we must let ourselves be guided by it. We can no longer do what we want, because this will coarsen and break the relationship. It is a life of total devotion. Of course it brings tremendous joy, love, helping and healing, and after a while we have no desire to go back to our earlier ways. But initially we must sacrifice those parts of our life that are not in line with love and service, and this can be hard. Nevertheless, it is the way we must all go eventually, and we can either climb the slow and winding or the steep and stony path. Don't despair, you travel at the pace that suits you.

I am trying to climb the steep path, but it isn't easy. I still have my weaknesses, and my indulgences – I can sob at a sad movie (who didn't watch *Greyfriars Bobby* and shed bucketfuls when the old hobo's dog was saved from being put down and instead given the freedom of the city of Edinburgh?) and I am a terrible chocoholic. I still enjoy my own company a bit too much for some of those around me – as I've said, I hardly ever socialize with the *Coronation Street* cast, indeed I don't even know where most of them live.

But I've learned that as we progress, we become more sensitive, and life in many respects seems harder. The thought of animals being slaughtered for you to eat becomes unbearable; the sight of people suffering rips you apart. Anger and hate seem like major illnesses. But it is only by going through all this that you will find out how strong you are. The spirit is stronger than anything on Earth and there is no power greater than the power of love.

I started out feeling afraid of death and infinity. Now I know there is no reason for either to be feared. Death is a change of environment, that's all. It is something to look forward to because it is a process that leads to a better life. And the fact that infinity goes on forever gives me a great feeling of peace and security. In fact, I love it. We are all infinite. We exist forever and ever and we are growing in love all the time. It's wonderful. Sadly, of course, that doesn't apply to Ken

Barlow – his end will come, although I hope he will live in people's memories for a while. But for William Roache and you, dear reader, life will go on, albeit it in a different place.

As we move forward, our aim should be to make ourselves little beacons of light and illuminate the area we're in. That way we make things better both for ourselves and for those around us. And when we reach a certain point, all we are interested in, all we want to do, is to help others.

I remember someone said to me once that an intensive course of self-development was selfish. That rocked me back a bit. He was absolutely right. It *is* selfish, but only in the initial stages. Later on, as you move forward, all you want to do is love and serve.

Unfortunately, we often need shocks and difficulties to wake us up. It's only by over-coming some form of suffering that we get the strength and the wisdom to move forward. The Earth is a hard school and it may seem a horrible place at times, but more and more people are now gaining a spiritual understanding and I feel sure that ultimately we will discharge all the darkness and move into a very beautiful age of peace and harmony.

I've already seen a big shift in people's attitudes in my own lifetime. In my younger days most people didn't think, for instance, about whether it was right to go to war or not. Your country was at war, so you went. You were a coward or a traitor if you thought otherwise. And if you had a nervous breakdown in the front line, you were shot. That attitude has totally changed now. People don't just blindly follow governments because they decide to go to war. Look at the opposition to the war in Iraq, for example.

So I'm very hopeful. There is still a lot of evil in the world, but there is also a wonderful enlightenment going on. Even films and television programmes have more of a spiritual side than they used to. Overall there's a swing in the right direction. We're breaking down national barriers and learning to live together. We're all brothers and sisters, after all; we're all equal in a spiritual sense, equal in love and equal in honour. We are all part of God.

So all you have to do is to tune in to your own soul. Let go and marvellous things will happen.

I wish you well on your journey; and remember, enjoy yourself.

A Gift of Understanding

You are very special. There is only one of you. God loves you and has appointed a Guardian Angel to be with you at all times.

You are a spiritual being first and foremost and as such you are immortal and indestructible. The essence of your spiritual being is divine love.

Temporarily you are incarnated in a physical vehicle or body and have left your real home in the spiritual realms so that you can learn and grow through the experience of the material world.

You are also given a mind and desires and it is up to you whether, through the mind, you control the body and desires or you let them control you. The first labour is to become the master of yourself.

So you are this wonderful creation of spirit, mind, emotions and body, and you are free to do whatever you want. Free to make choices, to discriminate between the polarities of this material world; love and hate, good and evil, reason and intuition, fear and trust, spiritual and physical.

You have free will but it is subject to a law. One law that applies throughout the entire universe, in the spiritual as well as the physical realms. It is inevitable, invariable and stands no abrogation. It is the law of cause and effect.

For good or ill you get back what you give out in thought, word and deed. You reap what you sow. Hate and you will attract hate, love and you will be loved.

The human condition is one of fallibility and imperfection and all the evil in the world has been created by man's free will serving his baser self.

On the road through your destiny there will be problems and suffering; remember these are but lessons and you will never be given more than you can bear; and your Guardian Angel will always hear your call for help. You will come through wiser and stronger as steel is tempered in the furnace.

You evolve on your journeys through many lives to a state of spiritual maturity that no longer requires the Earth school.

Your spirit is a passenger and will not intrude. But when the mind, emotions and body have been quietened and the spirit, or true self, is invited to take over, then you will be filled with a wonderful golden glow and know a joy like you have never known.

That is when you and your spirit have become one. The purpose of life.

Afterword

On meeting Bill for the first time, I was immediately attracted to his charismatic nature and genuine understanding of life. It can very often be difficult to describe a person whose mind is so open and expanded, but I would have to say that Bill has a magnetism that comes from the very highest part of his being.

I have been fortunate to share a platform with Bill, where we both spoke about our thoughts and beliefs of this life. I still remember being almost spellbound when I heard Bill describe his own understanding of life in the universe. All that he expressed could have come out of my own mind, but not with such eloquence.

Bill Roache, I believe, is a very compassionate man who knows where he fits in in the grand scale of life. His spiritual nature is such that – for all his great achievements and success in this life – he is very understated and genuinely humble. I feel honoured to have met a true gentleman of spirit.

Gordon Smith
Psychic and medium
August 2007

The publishers hope that this book has given you enjoyable reading. Large Print Books are especially designed to be as easy to see and hold as possible. If you wish a complete list of our books please ask at your local library or write directly to:

Magna Large Print Books
Magna House, Long Preston,
Skipton, North Yorkshire.
BD23 4ND

This Large Print Book, for people
who cannot read normal print,
is published under the auspices of

THE ULVERSCROFT FOUNDATION